TIMELESS STOICISM

Ancient Wisdom for Emotional Resilience, Unshakable Confidence, Inner Peace, and a Grounded Mindset for Success in Today's World - Learn Stimulating Exercises and Journaling Prompts

---

NOLAN VILLA

Copyright © 2024 by NOLAN VILA

All rights reserved.

No part of this book may be reproduced in any form or by any electronic or mechanical means, including information storage and retrieval systems, without written permission from the author, except for the use of brief quotations in a book review.

This publication is designed to provide accurate and authoritative information in regard to the subject matter covered.

It is sold with the understanding that neither the author nor the publisher is engaged in rendering legal, investment, accounting or other professional services.

While the publisher and author have used their best efforts in preparing this book, they make no representations or warranties with respect to the accuracy or completeness of the contents of this book and specifically disclaim any implied warranties of merchantability or fitness for a particular purpose.

No warranty may be created or extended by sales representatives or written sales materials.

The advice and strategies contained herein may not be suitable for your situation. You should consult with a professional when appropriate.

Neither the publisher nor the author shall be liable for any loss of profit or any other commercial damages, including but not limited to special, incidental, consequential, personal, or other damages.

Contents

Introduction	vii
1. THE STOIC ROOTS	1
The Birth of Stoicism: Zeno of Citium and His Philosophical Vision	1
Stoicism and The Roman Empire: Influence and Expansion	4
The Tenets of Stoicism: Core Principles and Virtues	7
The Stoic Triangle: Physics, Ethics, and Logic	10
2. THE FOUR CARDINAL VIRTUES FOR A FULFILLING LIFE	13
Courage: The Virtue of Bravery and Perseverance	13
Justice: The Virtue of Fairness and Right Action	16
Wisdom: The Virtue of Knowledge and Sound Judgment	18
Temperance: The Virtue of Moderation and Self-Restraint	21
3. THE STOIC MASTERS AND ECHOES OF ANCIENT WISDOM	25
Marcus Aurelius: The Philosopher King	26
Epictetus: The Former Slave Who Taught Freedom	30
Seneca: The Wealthy Statesman and His Moral Lessons	34
4. FINDING THE PATH TO EUDAIMONIA	41
The Stoic Definition of Happiness	41
Stoicism and Modern Psychology: The Role of Cognitive Behavioral Therapy	44
The Root of Unhappiness	47

Happiness Through Stoic Practices: Daily Exercises	49
Embrace Simplicity through Stoicism	52

5. BUILDING A GROUNDED MINDSET BRICK-BY-BRICK — 55

Stoicism and Mental Toughness: The Dichotomy of Control	56
Strategies for Building Resilience: A Stoic Approach	58
Stoicism and Resilience: Case Study	61
Building Resilience: Journaling Exercises	64

6. ACCEPTING THE UNCONTROLLABLE — 69

The Art of Acceptance	69
Techniques for Practicing Acceptance: Stoic Strategies	71
Stoicism and Acceptance: Case Study	74
Reflective Prompts for Acceptance: Journaling Exercises	76

7. UNLOCK UNSHAKABLE CONFIDENCE — 81

Confidence Through Stoic Eyes	81
Building Confidence: Stoic Techniques and Practices	83
Stoicism and Confidence: Case Study	86
Confidence Boosters: Journaling Exercises	88

8. MASTERING THE MODERN-DAY HUSTLE — 93

The Stoic Approach to Work and Career	94
Practical Stoic Techniques for the Workplace	96
Stoicism in The Modern Day: Case Study One	100
Stoicism in The Modern Day: Case Study Two	102

9. STOIC SECRETS FOR LASTING RELATIONSHIPS — 105

The Stoic Perspective on Relationships	105
Stoic Strategies for Healthy Relationships	108
Stoicism and Relationships: Case Study	111
Reflecting on Relationships: Journaling Exercises	114

10. LIVING MINDFULLY IN THE DIGITAL AGE	117
Stoicism in the Digital Age	117
Strategies for Digital Detox	120
What the Ancient Stoics Can Teach Us About the Digital Age	122
Digital Detox Prompts: Journaling Exercises	125
11. TURN YOUR SETBACKS INTO OPPORTUNITIES	129
The Stoic Approach to Failure and Setbacks	129
Turning Setbacks Into Opportunities: Case Study One	132
Turning Setbacks Into Opportunities: Case Study Two	135
Reflective Prompts for Overcoming Setbacks: Journaling Exercises	137
Epilogue	141
Resources	145

Introduction

In this frantic, fast-paced world where uncertainty is the only certainty and chaos often seems to reign, the philosophy of Stoicism provides an anchor. Stoicism, an ancient philosophy, might seem far removed from our modern realities, yet its principles are more relevant now than ever before. It offers a path to grounded confidence, resilience, acceptance, and happiness, which are all more than just desirable attributes; they are fundamentally necessary in our current times.

Stoicism is not about having a stiff upper lip or suppressing emotions. This philosophy can help you face challenges with poise, respond rather than react to life's curveballs, and lead a life of calm, compassion, and courage. It is about understanding what we can and cannot control and finding peace and purpose within that understanding.

The promise of Stoicism is immense. It offers a life that is not buffeted by external circumstances but navigated with internal clarity. It offers a life where confidence is not arrogance, resilience is not rigidity, acceptance is not resignation, and happiness is not fleeting pleasure but a deep-rooted contentment.

This book is your guide to that life. It is a journey through the principles of Stoicism, illustrated with stories of the great stoics who lived these principles. But more than history, it is a manual for modern life, with practical strategies and exercises you can apply in your everyday scenarios. It is a journey that combines the wisdom of the ancients with the insights of modern psychology to provide you with a robust toolkit to navigate life.

As we launch into this exploration of Stoicism, please keep an open mind. Be ready to challenge your preconceptions, explore new ideas, and engage in exercises that will take these ideas from the realm of theory to the realities of your life.

The journey ahead is a path to a more grounded, resilient, accepting, and happier you. It is a path to a life where chaos does not cause anxiety but invites action, challenges do not lead to despair but growth, and acceptance is not a burden but a liberation. Happiness is not an elusive dream but a lived reality.

Welcome to the journey. Welcome to the practice of Stoicism.

ONE

The Stoic Roots

The Birth of Stoicism: Zeno of Citium and His Philosophical Vision

Picture the bustling marketplaces of ancient Athens, filled with lively discussions and intellectual debates, a hub of philosophical ideas. This environment was the world in which Stoicism took root, born out of the mind of Zeno of Citium.

Zeno's Life and Journey to Philosophy

Born around 334 BC in Citium, a Greek colony in Cyprus, Zeno was initially a successful merchant, living a life far removed from philosophy. However, a shipwreck that resulted in the loss of his cargo led him to Athens, a turn of fate that would change not just his life but also the course of philosophical thought.

In Athens, Zeno chanced upon a book by Socrates and was so captivated by it that he was compelled to seek out a philosophical school to pursue further knowledge. This thirst for wisdom led him to Crates, a Cynic philosopher under whom Zeno studied for some years.

The Founding of The Stoic School

However, Zeno's intellectual curiosity needed to be satiated. He studied under numerous teachers, absorbing the teachings of the Cynics, Megarians, and Platonists. This eclectic education, combined with his own reflections, culminated in the birth of a new school of philosophy: Stoicism, named after the Stoa Poikile, or Painted Porch, where Zeno taught.

Zeno's school was unique. It was not confined to the intellectual elite or the scholarly inclined. Instead, it was open to everyone, irrespective of their social status, reflecting the Stoic belief in the universality of reason. Zeno's school was a place where people came to learn not just how to debate or how to reason but how to live.

Zeno's Teachings and Philosophical Ideas

Zeno's philosophy was relatively straightforward, as articulated in his numerous, albeit now lost, works. He proposed that the good life, the life worth living, was one lived in accordance with nature. To live according to nature, according to Zeno, was to live a life of virtue, for virtue was the highest good, and vice was the only evil.

This might seem simplistic or even restrictive, but delve deeper, and you will find a philosophy rich in nuance and profound implications. For Zeno, virtue was not an abstract concept or an ideal to strive for. It was a practical guide for living, a compass to navigate the complex seas of life.

Zeno divided virtue into four main categories: wisdom, courage, justice, and temperance. Wisdom was the understanding of what was good, bad, and indifferent. Courage was the resilience to hold on to this understanding in the face of adversity. Justice was the knowledge of how to distribute resources and behave towards others. Temperance was the ability to master one's desires and maintain balance.

Zeno's philosophy was not about renouncing the world or suppressing emotions. Instead, it was about understanding the world, our place in it, and how to act following this understanding. At its heart, it was a philosophy of empowerment, providing the tools to navigate life with resilience, poise, and virtue.

Think of Zeno's philosophy as a toolkit for life, much like a first-aid kit. Just as a first-aid kit equips you to deal with physical injuries, Zeno's philosophy equips you with the strategies to handle life's challenges, enabling you to cultivate resilience, acceptance, and happiness.

"Man conquers the world by conquering himself," Zeno proclaimed. This quote is the essence of Stoicism, a philosophy not of conquest and domination but of understanding and self-mastery. It is a philosophy that, over two millennia later, continues to provide guidance, solace, and, above all, practical strategies for a life well-lived.

As we delve deeper into the teachings of Stoicism, remember Zeno's journey from merchant to philosopher. It was a journey of not linear progress but exploration, reflection, and transformation. It is a journey open to all of us, no matter where we are in life. All it requires is an open mind, a willing heart, and the courage to question, explore, and grow.

So, as you turn the page, think of yourself not just as a reader but as a student of Stoicism, embarking on a journey of philosophical exploration and personal transformation, just like Zeno of Citium did all those years ago in the bustling marketplaces of ancient Athens.

Stoicism and The Roman Empire: Influence and Expansion

Stoicism was not confined to Athens or its immediate surroundings. Like a river finding its way to the ocean, Stoicism coursed through the ancient world, eventually reaching the shores of Rome, where it found fertile ground for expansion.

Stoicism's entry into Rome was neither immediate nor straightforward. It was introduced around the late 2nd century BC and was initially met with curiosity, skepticism, and even resistance. Yet, over time, this philosophy from Greece found acceptance, even admiration, among the Romans. What sparked this change?

Stoicism's Spread in Rome

The spread of Stoicism in Rome was mainly due to the practical nature of its teachings. Romans were a pragmatic people, valuing discipline, duty, and resilience. Stoicism, with its emphasis on virtue, self-control, and stability, resonated deeply with these Roman values.

Furthermore, the Stoic idea that every individual, irrespective of their social status, could achieve virtue and wisdom appealed to the Roman concept of citizenship and equality before the law. This universality of Stoicism, its accessibility to all, played a considerable role in its acceptance and spread across the varied strata of Roman society.

The Roman Stoics were not mere imitators of their Greek predecessors. They adapted Stoicism, integrating it with their own traditions and values, giving it a distinct Roman flavor. This adaptation, this Romanization of Stoicism, ensured its relevance and resilience, contributing to its influence and expansion in the empire.

Influence on Roman Leaders

Stoicism was not just a philosophy for the masses; it found favor among the Roman elite, including philosophers, politicians, and even emperors. This was primarily due to the Stoic emphasis on virtue, duty, and discipline, qualities highly prized by Roman leaders.

Prominent statesmen like Cato the Younger embraced Stoicism, embodying its principles in their public and private lives. Cato's unwavering commitment to virtue, courage in the face of adversity, and dedication to duty exemplify the Stoic ideal, demonstrating its practical application in positions of power and responsibility.

Perhaps the most famous Roman Stoic was not a statesman but an emperor - Marcus Aurelius. His personal writings, now known as "Meditations," provide a unique insight into the mind of a Stoic emperor. Here was a man who had the power to indulge in every conceivable luxury yet chose to lead a life of simplicity, duty, and virtue, guided by the principles of Stoicism.

Marcus Aurelius was not an exception. Other emperors, notably Epictetus' student Arrian, were also influenced by Stoicism. This influence of Stoicism on Roman leaders ensured its integration into the empire's political and social fabric, contributing to its longevity and influence.

Stoicism's Role in Roman Society

Stoicism's impact on Rome was not confined to its leaders. It permeated Roman society, influencing its laws, institutions, and culture. The Stoic principles of reason, virtue, and equality found expression in Roman law, contributing to its emphasis on justice, fairness, and citizenship.

Institutions like the Roman Senate, focusing on duty, discipline, and public service, mirrored Stoic values. Even Roman literature and art bear the imprint of Stoicism, reflecting its themes of resilience, acceptance, and the impermanence of life.

Stoicism's most significant impact was on the everyday life of the Romans. It offered a way to navigate life's complexities and uncertainties, find peace amid chaos, and cultivate resilience in the face of adversity. It was a guide, a compass, steering the Romans toward a life of virtue, fulfillment, and tranquility.

From the bustling marketplaces of Athens to the grandeur of Rome, Stoicism had traveled a long path, evolving, adapting, and expanding. Yet, at its core, it remained faithful to its original teachings - a philosophy for living a good life, a life of virtue, wisdom, and inner peace. It is a philosophy as relevant today as it was in the ancient world.

As we continue our exploration of Stoicism, let us carry with us the lessons from its journey, the wisdom from its teachings, and the inspiration from its practitioners. Remember that Stoicism is more than a philosophy; it is a way of life, a path to a better, more fulfilling life. A path open to all of us, right here, right now.

The Tenets of Stoicism: Core Principles and Virtues

Understanding The Dichotomy of Control

Life, as we know it, is a complex web of events, situations, and experiences. Some are within our control, while others lie beyond our reach. Recognizing this distinction is at the heart of Stoicism. This fundamental Stoic principle is known as the Dichotomy of Control.

The Dichotomy of Control is quite simple yet extraordinarily powerful. It states that some things are up to us and within our control, and others are not. Things within our control are our own opinions, desires, and aversions—in short, our actions. Everything else, including our bodies, material possessions, reputation, and status, is not within our control.

It might seem counterintuitive. After all, don't we have control over our bodies, possessions, and reputation? Not quite, according to the Stoics. While we can influence these things, we cannot control them entirely. Our bodies age and fall sick, our possessions can be stolen or destroyed, and rumors or lies can tarnish our reputation.

By understanding and accepting the Dichotomy of Control, we can focus our energy and attention on what we can control—our actions, our responses, our values—and let go of what we cannot.

The Stoic View of Emotions

Emotions play a vital part in our lives. They color our experiences, shape our responses, and often dictate our actions. But where do emotions fit in the Stoic philosophy?

Contrary to popular belief, Stoicism does not advocate the suppression of emotions. Instead, it offers a nuanced understanding of emotions and a practical approach to managing them.

Stoics view emotions as judgments or opinions we form about things that happen to us. For example, losing a prized possession might upset or anger us. According to Stoicism, these emotions are not caused by the loss itself but by the value we attach to the possession and the judgment we form about the loss.

Stoicism encourages us to examine our emotions, to understand their underlying judgments, and to question their validity. Doing so allows us to manage our emotions by suppressing them and changing our judgments.

The Role of Virtue in Stoic Philosophy

Virtue is a cornerstone of Stoic philosophy. But what exactly is virtue, and why is it so important?

For the Stoics, virtue is the highest good, the ultimate goal of life. It is the quality that defines a good person and a life well-lived.

However, virtue is not a single attribute or quality. It combines four cardinal virtues: wisdom, courage, justice, and temperance. Wisdom is the ability to discern what is truly important in life. Courage is the ability to face adversity with resilience and grit. Justice is the commitment to treat others with fairness and respect. Temperance is the practice of self-control and modesty.

Each of these virtues is interdependent and interconnected. Wisdom guides us to act with justice. Courage gives us the strength to practice temperance, and so on. Together, they form a holistic framework for living a virtuous life.

Living a virtuous life goes beyond merely adhering to a specific set of rules or aligning with societal expectations... It is about cultivating an inner compass, guided by reason and driven by the pursuit of virtue. It is about making choices that align with our values, taking actions that reflect our principles, and leading a life that resonates with our true selves.

These core tenets of Stoicism—the Dichotomy of Control, the Stoic view of emotions, and the role of virtue—form the foundation of this philosophy. They provide a roadmap for navigating life, a compass for making decisions, and a beacon for leading a fulfilling and meaningful life. They offer a practical, accessible, and transformative approach to personal growth and self-improvement. This approach has stood the test of time and inspires millions worldwide.

The Stoic Triangle: Physics, Ethics, and Logic

Stoicism, at its core, is a philosophical approach offering practical advice for living a meaningful and satisfying life. However, beneath its practicality lies a robust intellectual framework, a three-part structure often called the Stoic Triangle. This triangle consists of Physics, Ethics, and Logic. Each part of this triangle complements the others, forming a comprehensive system of thought that underpins the practical teachings of Stoicism.

Stoic Physics: Understanding The Natural World

Physics, in the context of Stoicism, goes beyond its modern scientific connotation. For the

Stoics, Physics encompassed the study of nature and the universe, the principles that governed them, and our place within them.

The Stoics viewed the universe as a rational, organized system where everything was interconnected and part of a larger whole. They believed in a divine reason or Logos that governed the universe, infusing it with order and purpose. This view of the universe as a rational, orderly system had profound implications for how they approached life.

For instance, the Stoic practice of living by nature stems from their understanding of the universe as a rational, ordered system. By aligning ourselves with this natural order by living rationally and virtuously, we fulfill our role in the cosmic scheme of things, leading to a life of harmony and fulfillment.

Stoic Ethics: Living a Virtuous Life

The second part of the Stoic Triangle is Ethics, which deals with the question of how we should live our lives. For the Stoics, the answer to this question was clear: we should live virtuously.

We have already discussed the Stoic concept of virtue as the highest good, the ultimate goal of life. Stoic Ethics expands on this idea, providing a framework for living a virtuous life. This framework revolves around the four cardinal virtues of wisdom, courage, justice, and temperance, which we discussed earlier.

Wisdom guides us to discern what is truly good (virtue) and what is truly bad (vice) and to remain indifferent to things that are neither (like wealth or reputation). Courage enables us to face adversity with resilience and fortitude to act rightly, even when difficult. Justice compels us to treat others fairly and respectfully, acknowledging their inherent worth. Furthermore, temperance teaches us to exercise self-restraint and moderation; it is the art of desiring only what is appropriate.

By cultivating these virtues, by making them the guiding principles of our actions, we align ourselves with nature, fulfilling our potential as rational social beings. It leads to a life of eudaimonia, a state of fulfillment, tranquility, and flourishing.

Stoic Logic: The Art of Reasoning

The third part of the Stoic Triangle is Logic. However, Stoic Logic is more than just rules of inference or principles of valid reasoning. It includes the study of knowledge, the nature of truth, and the criteria for rational judgment.

For the Stoics, Logic was a tool for discerning truth from falsehood, making rational judgments, and ultimately, living virtuously. They believed that by cultivating clear, rational thinking, we can avoid false beliefs and misguided desires, which are the root causes of emotional disturbances.

For instance, losing a prized possession might make us feel upset. However, upon closer examination, we might realize that our upset is based on the false belief that the possession was necessary for our happiness. We can alleviate our upset by correcting this false belief and understanding that the true source of happiness lies in virtue, not possessions. This is the practical application of Stoic Logic.

The Stoic Triangle of Physics, Ethics, and Logic provides a comprehensive framework for understanding Stoicism. It shows that Stoicism is not just a collection of practical teachings but a coherent system of thought grounded in a rational understanding of the universe (Physics), a commitment to virtue (Ethics), and the cultivation of clear, rational thinking (Logic).

As we explore the practical strategies of Stoicism in the following chapters, let us keep in mind this underlying intellectual framework. It will give us a deeper understanding of these strategies, enabling us to apply them more effectively.

So, be prepared to engage your mind as well as your heart, to reflect deeply as well as act decisively, and above all, to live not just wisely and virtuously but also rationally. After all, that is the Stoic way!

TWO

The Four Cardinal Virtues for a Fulfilling Life

Life is not a sprint but a marathon, a test of endurance, determination, and resilience. It is not about how fast we run or how high we climb but how well we bounce back when we stumble and fall. This is the essence of courage, the first virtue we will explore in our foray into Stoic philosophy.

Courage: The Virtue of Bravery and Perseverance

Understanding Stoic Courage

In the Stoic sense, courage extends beyond the physical bravery often depicted in movies or novels. It is not about facing down a foe on a battlefield or scaling a treacherous mountain peak. Stoic courage is about emotional resilience, moral courage, and the strength of character to uphold our principles, even when tested by adversity.

It is about facing life's trials with equanimity, about standing up for what is right, even when it is unpopular or inconvenient. It is about confronting our fears, insecurities, and doubts, not with bravado, but with a calm, composed mind and a firm, unwavering resolve. That is what Stoic courage looks like.

Examples of Courage in Stoic Teachings

One of the most compelling examples of Stoic courage comes from the life of the philosopher Epictetus. Born into slavery, Epictetus faced unimaginable hardships and injustices. However, he refused to let his circumstances define him. He focused on what was within his control - his beliefs, values, and his response to his circumstances. His courage lay not in resisting or rebelling against his condition but in maintaining his dignity and integrity, even in the face of adversity.

Another example of Stoic courage is the Roman Emperor Marcus Aurelius, who led his empire through multiple crises, including wars, famines, and plagues. While he could have easily succumbed to despair or defeatism, Marcus confronted these challenges with courage and resilience. His personal writings, known as "Meditations," reveal a man who, despite his power and privilege, struggled with the same fears and doubts that we all do. Nevertheless, he found the courage to face them, persevere, and fulfill his duties as a ruler and human being.

Practical Steps to Cultivate Courage

Cultivating Stoic courage involves both understanding and practice. Here are some practical steps to help you cultivate this essential virtue:

- *Reflect on Your Values:* Courage starts with knowing what you stand for. Reflect on your values, your principles, your beliefs. Ask yourself: What matters most to me? What do I stand for? What am I willing to fight for?

- *Face Your Fears:* Identify your fears, anxieties, and insecurities. Instead of avoiding them, confront them. Ask yourself: What am I afraid of? Why does this frighten me? How can I face this fear?

- *Practice Resilience:* Look for opportunities to challenge yourself, step out of your comfort zone, and face adversity. It could be something as simple as speaking up in a meeting, taking on a challenging project, or standing up for someone unfairly treated.

- *Meditate on Mortality:* One of the most potent Stoic exercises is the practice of memento mori, or "remember that you will die." It is not meant to be morbid or depressing but to remind us of our mortality, to help us appreciate the preciousness of life, and to inspire us to live courageously and authentically.

- *Journal Your Progress:* Keep a journal of your courage practice. Record your fears, your challenges, your triumphs, and your setbacks. Reflect on your experiences, learn from them, and use them to fuel your courage.

Remember, courage is not about never feeling fear or never facing adversity. It is about feeling fear, facing adversity, and acting following our values, principles, and authentic selves. That is Stoic courage. We can all cultivate that courage with practice, patience, and perseverance.

Justice: The Virtue of Fairness and Right Action

Understanding Stoic Justice

Justice, in the realm of Stoicism, takes a more extensive view than simply the retribution or reparation we often associate with the term in legal contexts. For the Stoics, justice is the cornerstone that helps maintain harmony in our communities and personal relationships. It encapsulates the ideals of fairness, kindness, understanding, and respect for all, irrespective of their status or background.

Stoic justice underscores the principle that every individual possesses an inherent dignity, a spark of the divine Logos or rationality, making them worthy of respect and fair treatment. It challenges us to look beyond our personal interests, to consider the welfare of others, and to make decisions not solely based on our benefit but on the larger good.

Stoic justice calls on us to be honest, to fulfill our duties and responsibilities, to honor our commitments, and to treat others not as means to our ends but as ends in themselves. It is about recognizing the interconnectedness of our existence, the shared humanity that binds us all, and acting in a way that upholds this interconnectedness, this shared humanity.

Examples of Justice in Stoic Teachings

Seneca, the Roman Stoic philosopher, serves as an enlightening example of Stoic justice. Despite being a wealthy statesman, Seneca spoke about the need to treat all people with respect and kindness. His letters are filled with advice on treating enslaved people—considered property at the time—as equals, deserving of the same respect and kindness as free men. His writings highlight the importance of empathy, understanding, and fairness in all interactions, reflecting the core Stoic principle of justice.

Marcus Aurelius, too, embodied Stoic justice in his role as the Roman Emperor. He strived to rule fairly, treating his subjects with respect, making decisions for the greater good, and always ensuring his actions aligned with the principles of justice. His personal writings reveal a leader deeply committed to pursuing justice, constantly reflecting on his actions and striving to ensure they were fair, honorable, and virtuous.

Practical Steps to Cultivate Justice

Cultivating Stoic justice requires both introspection and action. Here are some practical steps to help you build this crucial virtue:

- *Reflect on Your Actions:* Regularly assess your actions and decisions. Are they fair? Do they consider the welfare of others? Are they in line with your principles? Honest reflection can help you align your actions with the principle of justice.

- *Practice Empathy:* Try to understand others' perspectives. It not only fosters understanding but can also help you make fair decisions that consider everyone's interests.

- *Be Honest and Keep Your Commitments:* Honesty is fundamental to justice. Practice honesty in all your interactions. Also, honor your commitments, which reflects respect for others' time and effort.

- *Treat Everyone with Respect:* Remember the Stoic belief that every individual possesses inherent dignity. Treat everyone you encounter respectfully and kindly, regardless of their status or background.

- *Contribute to Your Community:* Look for ways to contribute to your community. It could be through volunteering, helping a neighbor, or any action that benefits others.

Remember, cultivating justice is not a one-time act but a life-long commitment. It requires constant practice, patience, and perseverance. Through this practice, you can build a more profound sense of fairness, improve your relationships, and contribute positively to your community. The power of Stoic justice lies within each of us, waiting to be realized.

Wisdom: The Virtue of Knowledge and Sound Judgment

Understanding Stoic Wisdom

If we think of life as a vast, unpredictable sea, then wisdom is the compass that guides us through its tumultuous waves. In the realm of Stoicism, wisdom holds a place of paramount importance. It is not just about accumulating facts or mastering skills; it is about discerning what truly matters in life and making well-informed, rational decisions based on that understanding.

Stoic wisdom involves recognizing the difference between what is within our control and what is not, between what is essential and what is superfluous, between what is virtuous and what is not. It is about understanding the true nature of things, stripping away our preconceptions, biases, and desires, and seeing things as they truly are.

For the Stoics, wisdom is also about applying our knowledge practically and meaningfully. It is about using our understanding to navigate life's complexities, face its challenges with resilience, build harmonious relationships, and lead a life of virtue. Stoic wisdom is both a compass and a rudder, guiding us through life and steering us toward virtue, tranquility, and fulfillment.

Examples of Wisdom in Stoic Teachings

If we seek examples of Stoic wisdom, we need look no further than Epictetus, the former slave-turned-philosopher. Despite his harsh early life, Epictetus profoundly understood life and human nature. His teachings, filled with practical wisdom, continue to resonate with people across the globe.

Epictetus taught that our happiness depends not on external things but on how we perceive and respond to them. He encouraged us to focus on what is within our control and to let go of what is not. He says, "It is not what happens to you, but how you react to it that matters." This quote reflects the essence of Stoic wisdom - the ability to decide what truly matters and to act accordingly.

Another embodiment of Stoic wisdom is the Roman Emperor Marcus Aurelius. His Meditations, a collection of personal writings, provide a glimpse into a man's mind who sought wisdom above all else despite his power and wealth. He reflected on life's impermanence, virtue's importance, and the value of rational judgment. His writings, filled with profound insights and practical wisdom, continue to inspire people to lead a life of wisdom, virtue, and fulfillment.

Practical Steps to Cultivate Wisdom

While wisdom is often associated with age or experience, it is not confined to the elderly or the learned. Wisdom can be cultivated like a seed that, with care and patience, can grow into a sturdy tree. Here are some practical steps to help you cultivate Stoic wisdom:

- *Question Your Beliefs:* Our beliefs often shape our perceptions and decisions. We can better understand ourselves and the world around us by questioning our beliefs.

- *Seek Diverse Perspectives:* Wisdom often comes from seeing things from different perspectives. Seek out diverse viewpoints, engage with people from different backgrounds, and be open to new ideas and experiences.

- *Embrace Uncertainty:* Life is full of uncertainties. Instead of fearing them, embrace them. Uncertainty is a sign that we are stepping out of our comfort zone, exploring new territories, and growing wiser.

- *Practice Mindfulness:* Mindfulness is the art of being completely present in the moment. It can enhance our understanding of ourselves and our surroundings. It can help us see things as they truly are, free from our biases, judgments, or preconceptions.

- *Apply Your Knowledge:* Wisdom is not just about knowing but about doing. Apply your knowledge in your daily life. Use it to make well-informed decisions, to solve problems, and to navigate life's challenges.

These steps, while simple, can help you cultivate wisdom, one of the four cardinal virtues of Stoicism. Remember, wisdom is not a destination but a journey. It is not about reaching a state of perfect knowledge or understanding but about continually learning, growing, and evolving. It is about using our knowledge, understanding, and experiences to lead a life of virtue, tranquility, and fulfillment. This is the goal of Stoic wisdom, which is within reach of all of us.

Temperance: The Virtue of Moderation and Self-Restraint

Understanding Stoic Temperance

In a world that often champions excess, the virtue of temperance might seem out of place, even outdated. However, it is precisely in such a world that the need for temperance is most acute.

Temperance, from the Stoic perspective, is not about abstinence or austerity. It is about balance, moderation, and self-restraint. It is about understanding our needs, distinguishing them from our wants, and choosing not to be swayed by the latter.

Stoic temperance invites us to question our desires, examine their roots, and discern their worthiness. It encourages us to exercise self-control, to resist the allure of instant gratification, and to value long-term fulfillment over fleeting pleasure.

At its core, Stoic temperance is about freedom—the freedom from the tyranny of insatiable desires, the freedom to choose our actions wisely, and the freedom to lead a balanced, contented life.

Examples of Temperance in Stoic Teachings

When we look for embodiments of Stoic temperance, the figure of Epictetus once again comes to the fore. Epictetus demonstrated remarkable self-restraint and contentment despite his humble background and hardships. He did not yearn for wealth or status but found fulfillment in leading a simple, virtuous life.

Another exemplar of Stoic temperance is the Roman Emperor Marcus Aurelius. As the ruler of the Roman Empire, he had access to unimaginable wealth and luxury. However, his personal writings reveal a man who valued simplicity over extravagance, practiced self-restraint amidst abundance, and chose moderation over excess.

Practical Steps to Cultivate Temperance

Cultivating Stoic temperance requires both mindfulness and discipline. Here are some steps to help you foster this vital virtue:

- *Assess Your Desires:* Regularly take stock of your desires. Ask yourself: Do I need this or merely want it? Is this desire in line with my values? Is it beneficial for my long-term well-being?

- *Practice Self-Restraint:* Look for opportunities to exercise self-control. It could be as simple as resisting the need to check your phone every minute, opting for a healthy meal over junk food, or choosing to save money instead of making an impulsive purchase.

- *Cultivate Contentment:* Contentment is a crucial aspect of temperance. Practice gratitude for what you have, find joy in simple pleasures, and learn to be content with enough.

- *Mindful Consumption:* Be mindful when you consume, not just regarding food but also information, entertainment, and social interactions. Choose quality over quantity, substance over superficiality.

- *Slow Down:* In our fast-paced world, slowing down can be a powerful act of temperance. Take time to savor your experiences, to engage fully in your activities, and to appreciate the richness of the present moment.

Cultivating temperance is not about restricting your life but about enhancing it. It is about making wise choices, balancing your needs with your wants, and finding fulfillment in simplicity and moderation. This is the beauty of Stoic temperance, which, with practice, can bloom in our lives.

We have now explored the four cardinal virtues of Stoicism—courage, justice, wisdom, and temperance. These virtues provide a robust framework for leading a fulfilling life. They guide us in navigating life's challenges, building harmonious relationships, and finding contentment amidst our modern world's chaos.

As we proceed forward, we will delve deeper into the practical aspects of Stoicism, uncovering strategies and exercises to integrate these virtues into our daily lives. The road ahead is filled with insights, inspiration, and opportunities for growth. Let us continue to walk it together, guided by the wisdom of the Stoics and fueled by your desire for a more fulfilling life.

THREE

The Stoic Masters and Echoes of Ancient Wisdom

When faced with a world of profound indifference, the philosophy of Stoicism seeks to provide its adherents with a toolkit to ensure they can cope with the world's adversity. However, Stoicism is not just about coping with life's challenges. It is about thriving in this world of indifference.

Stoicism encompasses ancient wisdom, but it is highly personalized to its adherents. Stoicism is not an ideology but a set of maxims gleaned from the experiences of wise men and women. When we read the works of the Stoics, we interpret not only what these thinkers said but how their lives affected their teachings. Stoicism is an extension of the practice of life. So, we have to ask ourselves: Did the Stoics live life well? Did they live following their teachings?

In Stoicism, three figures stand out as embodying the core principles of this ancient philosophy—however imperfectly, a human being can embody their own values. These thinkers are beacons who guide us through the often turbulent seas of life.

Their wisdom, preserved in their writings, offers us insights, inspiration, and invaluable lessons for leading a virtuous, fulfilling life. The first of these lighthouses we explore is Marcus Aurelius—the philosopher king.

Marcus Aurelius: The Philosopher King

Marcus Aurelius's Life and Reign

Imagine ruling an empire, holding the fate of millions in your hands while grappling with the constant demands of leadership, the ever-present threat of war, and the relentless scrutiny of your subjects. Imagine doing all this while remaining steadfastly committed to virtue, wisdom, and self-improvement. This was the life of Marcus Aurelius, the man who served as Emperor of Rome and held his reign from AD 161 until 180.

Born into a prominent Roman family, Aurelius was adopted by the emperor Antoninus Pius at a young age. This twist of fate set him on the path to the throne, a path he walked with a philosopher's steadiness rather than a monarch's pomp. Aurelius faced numerous challenges during his reign, including wars on the empire's frontiers, a devastating plague, and internal conspiracies. Nevertheless, he navigated these challenges—not with despotism or despair but with wisdom and an unwavering commitment to his Stoic principles.

Key Teachings from Meditations

Much of what we know about Aurelius' Stoic beliefs comes from his personal writings, now known as *Meditations*. These writings were not intended for publication but were Aurelius' reflections and attempts to apply Stoic principles in his life and reign.

Meditations is a treasure trove of Stoic wisdom. It emphasizes the importance of understanding the nature of the universe and our place in it, focusing on what is within our control, accepting what is not, and cultivating virtues like wisdom, justice, courage, and temperance. Aurelius reminds us that everything happens because the Gods ordain it. He says,

> "What we ascribe to fortune happens not without a presiding nature, nor without a connection and intertexture with the things ordered by providence" (2.3).

Things happen for a reason, and all other things flow from our realization of that fact.

Life is hard, according to the Stoics, yet it is necessary—perhaps you agree with them! Aurelius states,

> "Consider, too, the necessity of these events and their utility to that whole universe of which you are a part" (2.3).

Aurelius continues,

> "Say thus to thyself every morning: today I may have to do with some intermeddler in other men's affairs, with an ungrateful man; an insolent, or a crafty, or an envious, or an unsociable selfish man." (2.1).

Furthermore, that is just to start! The solution for Aurelius is to conduct yourself with the qualities of a Roman—a man or virtuous individual—who shows genuine dignity, compassion, independence, and fairness. This approach, according to Aurelius, will liberate your mind from your worries and focus it on the betterment of yourself and your community.

One of Aurelius' most profound teachings is the concept of viewing life objectively, stripped of our biases, attachments, and fears. According to Aurelius, the universe is a harmonious whole, and we choose to act under this harmony. No one, says Aurelius, has the power to stop you from acting alongside nature because you, too, are part of nature. He encourages us to see things as they are, not as we want them to be. Clear-mindedness, he argues, frees us from unnecessary distress, helping us respond to life's challenges with composure, stating,

> "Quit your books: Be no longer distracted with different views. You have it in your own power" (2.2).

He adds, pointing out the power of us to change our reality,

> "Take away opinion, and you have removed the complaint, 'I am hurt.' Remove 'I am hurt,' and you remove the harm" (4.7).

Aurelius suggests that we are all, perhaps tragically so, the same:

> "My kinsmen...[are] not of the same blood or seed, but of the same intelligent divine part; and that I cannot be hurt by any of them since none of them can involve me in anything dishonorable or deformed. I cannot be angry at my kinsmen or hate them" (2.1).

Given this realization of sameness, Aurelius highlights the importance of living in the present moment—no matter who you are. As before,

> "If a man observes these things, the Gods require no more of him" (2.5).

Aurelius reminds us that the past is unchangeable, the future is uncertain, and the present is all we truly have. We can make do with this. We can turn coping into thriving. As Aurelius points out, a characteristic of the universe is that it transforms and harnesses anything that appears to resist or contradict it. Similarly, every human being has the ability to perceive any obstacle in its path as an opportunity for personal action. You can turn a challenge into an opportunity, just like the universe does.

In short, by focusing on the present, we can live fully, act virtuously, and find tranquility amidst life's inevitable turbulence.

Influence of Marcus Aurelius on Stoicism

Though known as one of the "good" Roman emperors, Aurelius' reign was marred by war and famine. One can say that Aurelius was dealt a "bad hand" and made the best of it by applying Stoic doctrine.

Aurelius' impact on Stoicism is immeasurable. Through his writings, he introduced Stoicism to countless individuals, providing them with practical guidance for leading virtuous and fulfilling lives. While *Meditations* was not published during his lifetime, Aurelius' work was received by Renaissance thinkers, Enlightenment philosophers, and even America's founding fathers. Moreover, Aurelian Stoicism is popular today as a philosophical school and a basis for psychotherapy. The emperor's own life stands as a testament to the applicability of Stoic principles across various domains.

The teachings of Aurelius continue to resonate with the general public, with *Meditations* at the forefront of most readers' introduction to Stoicism. Aurelius' *Meditations* underscores the importance of objectivity, living in the present, and the transformative power of virtue. His writings, characterized by wisdom, humility, and a profound understanding of human nature, are a lighthouse directing the ship of our lives toward virtue, tranquility, and fulfillment.

As you read on, recall Aurelius, the Roman emperor who chose the path of philosophy over the trappings of power. Remember his teachings, his wisdom, his resilience. Moreover, note that, like Aurelius, we too can choose the path of philosophy—the path of Stoicism—which will lead us towards a life of virtue, tranquility, and fulfillment.

Epictetus: The Former Slave Who Taught Freedom

Epictetus' Life Story

The Roman Empire was a pragmatic political system encapsulating many diverse ethnicities and religions. The intellectual activity of the Roman Empire was massive, and Stoicism is but one philosophical school within it. Nevertheless, Stoicism fit the Roman Empire's prevailing ideology like a glove. This is partly because life for Romans was hard, and they desperately needed strategies to cope with and transcend their situation. No more evident example of this is Epictetus, a slave-turned-philosopher, who argued that one must accept one's situation —even if one is a slave.

Born around 50 AD, Epictetus was a slave in the household of Epaphroditos, a wealthy freedman and secretary to the Roman Emperor Nero. Despite his harsh circumstances, Epictetus discovered a passion for philosophy. With his master's permission, he studied under Musonius Rufus, a renowned Stoic philosopher. These studies laid the foundation for his future teachings and formed the bedrock of his Stoic beliefs.

Epictetus gained his freedom after Emperor Nero's death and began teaching philosophy in Rome. However, when Emperor Domitian banished philosophers from Rome, Epictetus moved to Nicopolis in Greece, where he established a school. Here, he spent the rest of his life teaching, writing, and living the principles of Stoicism.

Key Teachings from the Discourses and the Enchiridion

Epictetus did not pen any books himself. Instead, his teachings were recorded and preserved by his student, Arrian. These writings, known as the Discourses and the Enchiridion, capture the essence of Epictetus's Stoic philosophy.

The Discourses consist of eight books, although only four survive today. They contain Epictetus' teachings in the form of dialogues and discussions, covering various topics from ethics to philosophy of mind. Central to these teachings is the Stoic doctrine of the dichotomy of control—the idea that some things are within our control while others are not. As Epictetus states,

"Happiness and freedom begin with a clear understanding of one principle; Some things are within our control, and some things are not." (Epictetus & Lebell, 1995, p. 43).

He urges his students to focus on what they can control—their actions, judgments, and desires—and to accept what they cannot—their bodies, possessions, and social status. Epictetus emphasizes that,

"No man is free who is not a master of himself" (Atkins, 2017).

The Enchiridion, or "Handbook," is a condensed version of the Discourses. It provides practical advice for leading a Stoic life, focusing on applying philosophical principles in everyday situations. Epictetus advises,

"Do not demand or expect that events happen as you would wish them to. Accept events as they actually happen. That way, peace is possible." (Epictetus & Lebell, 1995, p. 23)

He recognizes that external events are beyond our control, but our internal reactions and attitudes are within our power. Epictetus taught,

"It is not what happens to you, but how you react to it that matters." ("Epictetus quotes," n.d.)

The Enchiridion emphasizes the importance of internal freedom—the freedom that comes from understanding the dichotomy of control, accepting the world as it is, and cultivating virtue. As Epictetus suggests,

> "If you want to develop your ability to live simply, do it for yourself, do it quietly, and do not do it to impress others." (Epictetus & Lebell, 1995, p. 80).

He encourages his students to focus on self-improvement and not to be swayed by external judgments. Epictetus's teachings remind us,

> "First say to yourself what you would be, and then do what you have to do." ("Epictetus quotes," n.d.).

It is through this self-reflection and aligned action that we can find true fulfillment.

Epictetus' Influence on Stoic Philosophy

Epictetus had a significant and wide-ranging impact on philosophy. For instance, Marcus Aurelius expresses gratitude to his teacher, Junius Rusticus, for introducing him to Epictetus. Rusticus may have attended Epictetus' lectures and passed on his notes to Marcus. However, it is more likely that Marcus read the widely circulated notes by Arria.

Through his writings, Epictetus gave Stoicism a distinctly practical orientation. He turned philosophy into a daily living guide and personal transformation tool. His teachings offer timeless wisdom on leading a virtuous, fulfilling life. They remind us that our happiness depends not on external circumstances but on our internal attitudes, judgments, and actions.

James Stockdale, who endured over seven years as a prisoner of war in Vietnam, credits Epictetus for providing him with a framework to withstand the tortures he experienced (Stockdale, 2001). While being confined in leg irons, Stockdale likely remembered that Epictetus himself had a disabled leg, potentially broken by his master. Epictetus, however, taught that illness hinders the body but not one's ability to choose, and the same applies to physical impairments. By adopting this perspective, Stockdale viewed obstacles as hindrances to something external rather than to himself.

Epictetus's influence extends beyond the realm of philosophy. His teachings have inspired cognitive-behavioral therapy (CBT), a modern form of psychotherapy that helps individuals change unhelpful beliefs and behaviors. His emphasis on accepting what we cannot control and focusing on what we can control connects deeply with the principles of CBT today.

From the slave quarters of Rome to the lecture halls of Nicopolis, Epictetus' life was a living embodiment of Stoicism. His teachings, brimming with wisdom, courage, and resilience, continue to light the path for those seeking a virtuous, fulfilling life. As we delve deeper into the world of Stoicism, let us carry forth Epictetus' teachings—reminding ourselves of the freedom that comes from understanding the dichotomy of control, from accepting the world as it is, and from cultivating virtue.

Seneca: The Wealthy Statesman and His Moral Lessons

Seneca's Life and Career

It is not so easy to be a Stoic! That is the whole point: the difficulty of life necessitates Stoicism. However, once you are a practicing Stoic, no one would be a Stoic if it is not possible to succeed in life.

The story of Seneca—a man of paradoxes—illustrates the difficulty of having fidelity to a belief system like Stoicism, even though Seneca was a pivotal figure in the annals of Stoic philosophy. He was a statesman of considerable wealth, and yet his words echoed the virtues of simplicity and self-restraint. Some commentators criticized this apparent contradiction as hypocrisy or opportunism on the part of Seneca (Wilson, 2015). In reality, Seneca reminds us that no one is perfect in their conduct (despite this, he had some quite "Stoic" moments, especially near his death) in our pursuit of a belief system like Stoicism. Let us cast our gaze on the life of Lucius Annaeus Seneca—better known as Seneca the Younger.

Born into a prominent Roman family in the 1st century AD, Seneca was educated in Rome and Athens, where he was introduced to Stoicism. A man of letters and politics, Seneca navigated the corridors of power as an advisor to Emperor Nero. This position brought him both influence and wealth, but it also embroiled him in the political intrigues of the era. Political intrigue is somewhat of a neutral term, though; Nero was a deranged and insane emperor who ordered Seneca to death by suicide. Being a good Roman, Seneca complied. Seneca's drinking of the hemlock while reciting Stoic poetry is among the most iconic moments of Ancient philosophy, right next to Socrates' own death through hemlock, as recounted by Plato.

Despite his engagement with the material world, to the point of extravagant wealth, Seneca remained steadfastly devoted to his Stoic principles. He walked the tightrope between his public life and philosophical beliefs: a balancing act defining his legacy.

Key Teachings from Letters from a Stoic

Seneca left behind a rich body of work, but his *Letters from a Stoic* holds a special place in Stoic literature. These letters, written to his friend Lucilius, encapsulate his philosophy and offer practical guidance for leading a virtuous life. Seneca remarks,

> "You want to live—but do you know how to live? You are scared of dying—and, tell me, is the kind of life you lead really any different from being dead?" (Seneca & Campbell, 1969, p. 58)

In his letters, Seneca presents a clear-eyed view of life's trials and tribulations:

> "What good does it do you to go overseas," he muses, "to move from city to city? If you really want to escape the things that harass you, what you are needing is not to be in a different place but to be a different person" (Seneca & Campbell, 1969, p. 85).

He counsels acceptance of life's ups and downs, advocating peace of mind through understanding and virtue. Philosophy allows us to gain harmony with our minds and nature. He encourages us to focus our efforts on self-improvement and moral fortitude rather than chasing fleeting pleasures or social status, writing,

> "Until we have begun to go without them, we fail to realize how unnecessary many things are" (Seneca & Campbell, 1969, p. 104).

These "things" include our material possessions. According to Seneca, we are more motivated by our desire to look good to others rather than our employment of reason.

Seneca also underscores the importance of time, urging us to be mindful of its fleeting nature. He writes,

> "Life is long enough, and a sufficiently generous amount has been given to us for the highest achievements if it were all well invested. However, when it is wasted in heedless luxury and spent on no good activity, we are forced at last by death's final constraint to realize that it had passed away before we knew it was passing. So it is: we are not given a short life, but we make it short, and we are not ill-supplied but wasteful of it….Life is long if you know how to use it." (Popova, 2014)

Seneca cautions against wasting our time on trivial pursuits and exhorts us to make the most of the present moment, stating,

> "People are frugal in guarding their personal property; but as soon as it comes to squandering time, they are most wasteful of the one thing in which it is right to be stingy" (Popova, 2014).

While life is short, it is upon us to live it well and philosophically, according to Seneca.

Seneca's Influence on Stoic Philosophy

Seneca's profound influence on Stoic philosophy and his significant contributions to our understanding of it are widely recognized. His writings have served as guiding lights for countless seekers of wisdom, providing valuable insights into the art of leading a virtuous life.

Contrary to the notion that Stoicism is solely for those who renounce the world, Seneca's life is a reminder that Stoic principles are equally applicable to individuals actively engaged in society. He demonstrated that Stoicism can harmoniously coexist with public life if one upholds one's principles.

Seneca's philosophy offers a nuanced interpretation of Stoicism—embracing the intricacies of human existence without compromising the fundamental tenets of the school. His teachings continue to resonate with us, underscoring the significance of virtue, the value of time, and the transformative power of acceptance.

Furthermore, Seneca's intellectual range extends far beyond his moral philosophy. In addition to his essays on practical matters such as mortality, adversity, anger, leisure, tranquility, and happiness, he delved into various topics in the natural sciences, exploring rivers, thunder and lightning, earthquakes, and comets.

Additionally, Seneca produced an extensive body of dramatic works. His most famous work remains his extensive correspondence with Lucilius: *Letters to a Stoic*. The breadth of his contributions to moral philosophy, science, and literature would rightfully earn him the designation of a polymath. However, despite his remarkable achievements, Seneca has not always received the widespread acclaim he deserves.

Throughout the Middle Ages and the Renaissance, Seneca enjoyed a more relatively glowing reputation. In one striking medieval miniature found in a manuscript containing philosophical texts, Seneca is prominently placed at the center—flanked by Plato and Aristotle. Esteemed scholars of the time, such as Peter Abelard in the twelfth century and Francesco Petrarch two hundred years later, hailed Seneca as the greatest moral philosopher and teacher. The University of Piacenza in Italy even established a Chair in Seneca Studies. Seneca, along with Cicero, profoundly influenced the early Humanists' worldview. Erasmus, who edited printed editions of Seneca's works in the sixteenth century, remarked that

> "Anyone who reads him with a desire for improvement will be left a better man" (Sellars, 2019).

In the grand sea of history and philosophy, figures like Marcus Aurelius, Epictetus, and Seneca are beacons of wisdom—illuminating our way through life's tumultuous currents. These philosophers embody the principles of Stoicism, not only in their teachings but also in the very fabric of their existence. They offer us invaluable guidance for cultivating a virtuous and meaningful life.

As we venture further into Stoicism, we will embark on a profound exploration of its practical dimensions. In this journey, we will also unveil strategies and exercises designed to help us integrate these timeless principles into our daily lives. Let us persist in our quests for knowledge, introspection, and personal growth—drawing profound inspiration from the lives and teachings of these Stoic masters. Together, we will navigate the path of Stoicism, forging ahead toward lives of virtue, tranquility, and fulfillment.

FOUR

Finding The Path to Eudaimonia

Imagine standing at the foot of a giant mountain, looking up at the peak shrouded in mist. You know the climb will be challenging, but you are drawn to the promise of the view from the top. Now, imagine if the climb itself could be as fulfilling as the view, if every step, every breath, every bead of sweat could be a source of contentment. This is the vision of happiness in Stoic philosophy—a journey that is as rewarding as the destination.

The Stoic Definition of Happiness

Eudaimonia: The Stoic Ideal

In the Stoic vocabulary, the word for happiness is 'eudaimonia,' a Greek term that translates to 'good spirit' or 'flourishing.' But eudaimonia is more than just a fleeting sense of joy or a momentary pleasure. It's akin to the deep-rooted contentment a tree derives from being firmly planted in nourishing soil, its branches reaching out to the sky, its leaves dancing in the wind. Eudaimonia is about flourishing as a human being and leading a fulfilling, meaningful life.

How does one achieve eudaimonia? According to the Stoics, the path to eudaimonia lies not in the pursuit of pleasure or the avoidance of pain but in the cultivation of virtue. Much like a tree that thrives not by chasing the sunlight but by sinking its roots deep into the ground, we flourish not by chasing external goods but by cultivating our inner character.

Virtue as the Sole Good

In the eyes of a Stoic, virtue is the sole good—the ultimate measure of a life well-lived. In this context, virtue refers to the four cardinal virtues of wisdom, courage, justice, and temperance. Wisdom guides us to act rightly, courage enables us to face adversity with equanimity, justice ensures we treat others fairly, and temperance helps us maintain balance in our desires.

Think of these virtues as the four cardinal points on a compass guiding us on our journey to eudaimonia. They provide direction when we are lost, offer clarity when we are confused, and give us strength when we are weary. With these virtues as our guide, we can navigate life's ups and downs with resilience, stability, and grace.

But what about wealth, health, reputation, and other external goods? Aren't they essential for happiness? Not necessarily, according to the Stoics.

Indifference to External Circumstances

Stoicism tells us to be indifferent to external circumstances—to view them as neither good nor bad but simply as facts of life. It does not mean we should neglect our health or disregard our wealth. It simply means we should not attach our happiness to these external goods.

Imagine you are a sailor setting off on a voyage. You cannot control the wind or the waves, but you can control how you set your sail and navigate your ship. Similarly, we cannot control what happens to us, but we can control how we respond to them and guide our lives.

By focusing on the things we can control—our actions, attitudes, and virtues—we free ourselves from the tyranny of external circumstances. We empower ourselves to lead a life of virtue, to navigate our path to eudaimonia, regardless of the wind, waves, trials, or tribulations.

This is the Stoic definition of happiness—a state of flourishing that arises from living a life of virtue, focusing on what is within our control, and being indifferent to external circumstances. It is a definition that's both challenging and empowering, that calls us to rise above our circumstances, cultivate our virtues, and seize the reins of our happiness.

In the words of Epictetus,

> "Do not seek for everything to happen as you wish it would, but rather wish that everything happens as it actually will—then your life will flow well."

As we continue our exploration of Stoicism, let us carry these insights with us. Let us strive to cultivate virtue, focus on what is within our control, and embrace indifference toward external circumstances. In doing so, we can set sail on our voyage to eudaimonia, guided by the wisdom of the Stoics and fueled by our own inner strength.

Stoicism and Modern Psychology: The Role of Cognitive Behavioral Therapy

Stoic Roots of CBT

Stoicism, emphasizing self-control, acceptance, and the transformation of perceptions, has been a significant source of inspiration for modern psychological therapies, particularly Cognitive Behavioral Therapy (CBT). CBT, developed in the mid-20th century by Dr. Aaron T. Beck, is a kind of psychotherapy that can help identify and change negative thought loops that lead to harmful behaviors and emotions.

CBT's central premise, much like Stoicism, is that our thoughts, not external events, determine our feelings and behaviors. This concept echoes the Stoic principle articulated by Epictetus:

> "Men are disturbed not by things, but by the views which they take of them."

In other words, it's not what happens to us that causes distress but how we interpret and respond to what happens.

By helping individuals recognize and challenge their negative thoughts, CBT enables them to change their behaviors and emotions, improving their mental health and overall well-being. This type of therapy aligns closely with the Stoic practice of examining and questioning our judgments to manage our emotions and live more virtuously.

Rational Emotive Behavior Therapy (REBT)

Another modern psychological approach influenced by Stoicism is Rational Emotive Behavior Therapy (REBT), which Dr. Albert Ellis developed in the 1950s. REBT, like CBT, focuses on identifying and changing limiting beliefs that lead to emotional and behavioral problems.

The parallels between REBT and Stoicism are striking. Both emphasize the role of rational judgment in managing emotions and behavior. Both advocate for acceptance of what is beyond our control. And both promote the cultivation of virtue, particularly wisdom and temperance, for leading a fulfilling life.

For instance, REBT uses a technique called 'disputing' to challenge irrational beliefs. REBT involves questioning the evidence for the belief, the usefulness of the belief, and the logical consistency of the belief. It mirrors the Stoic practice of examining our judgments, questioning their validity, and replacing them with more rational ones.

Mindfulness-Based Cognitive Therapy (MBCT)

Another therapy that shares common ground with Stoicism is Mindfulness-Based Cognitive Therapy (MBCT). Developed by Zindel Segal, Mark Williams, and John Teasdale, MBCT combines elements of cognitive therapy with mindfulness techniques to help people better understand and manage their thoughts and emotions.

Mindfulness, the practice of being fully present and engaged in the current moment, aligns closely with the Stoic principle of living following nature. By focusing on the present, we align ourselves with the natural flow of life, freeing ourselves from the regrets of the past and anxieties about the future.

MBCT encourages us to observe our thoughts and feelings without judgment or resistance, much like the Stoic practice of viewing life objectively. This mindful observation allows us to see our thoughts and feelings for what they are—temporary and subjective experiences, not absolute truths or permanent states.

Integrating mindfulness with cognitive therapy, MBCT helps individuals respond to negative thoughts and feelings more adaptively, reducing their impact and improving mental well-being. It reflects the Stoic goal of tranquility—a state of inner peace achieved through understanding, acceptance, and virtuous living.

From the Stoic roots of CBT to the commonalities with REBT and MBCT, it's clear that Stoicism has profoundly influenced modern psychology. These therapies, grounded in Stoic principles, offer practical tools for managing thoughts, emotions, and behaviors, leading to improved mental health and well-being.

Nevertheless, they also underscore the timeless relevance of Stoic philosophy. The same principles that guided Marcus Aurelius, Epictetus, and Seneca—rational judgment, acceptance, and virtue—are helping people today navigate life's challenges, manage their mental health, and lead more fulfilling lives.

So, as you explore Stoicism, remember that you are not just engaging with an ancient philosophy but with a living tradition

—a tradition that has shaped, and continues to help shape, our understanding of the mind, our approach to mental health, and our pursuit of a good life.

The Root of Unhappiness

Seneca, the esteemed Stoic philosopher, profoundly stated,

> "It is not the man who has too little but the man who craves more, that is poor." (Seneca & R. Campbell, 2004, Letters from a Stoic)

This poignant observation strikes at the heart of a prevalent cause of dissatisfaction in life: the relentless pursuit of more, irrespective of our existing possessions and circumstances.

This widespread misconception — that happiness is a destination reached by acquiring certain statuses or possessions — is deeply ingrained in societal narratives. Common beliefs suggest that escaping the constraints of parental authority, achieving wealth, fame, or power, or finding the ideal romantic partner will end loneliness and resolve all of life's difficulties. Psychologists refer to this as 'conditional happiness,' a never-ending chase after a goal always just beyond reach, much like an elusive horizon.

Epictetus, another influential voice in Stoicism, asserted the futility of seeking happiness while longing for that which we do not have. He believed that genuine happiness is found in contentment with one's current state, akin to the satisfaction of someone who is well-nourished and feels neither hunger nor thirst.

To truly overcome the barriers to happiness, one must recognize and confront this insatiable desire for more to overcome the obstacles. Stoic philosophy teaches the value of choosing contentment and gratitude over perpetual yearning, as these states are fundamentally at odds.

Let's delve deeper into practical examples of how Stoicism can guide us in various aspects of life:

- *Career Ambitions:* Consider an individual fixated on the next career milestone, convinced it will bring fulfillment. Stoicism suggests deriving satisfaction from one's present professional situation, emphasizing personal development and meaningful contributions over mere job titles. This approach fosters a sense of accomplishment and purpose in the current role rather than in some elusive future position.

- *Financial Objectives:* Reflect on the notion that accumulating a certain amount of wealth will result in happiness. Stoicism encourages us to cherish and maximize our present financial situation, finding delight in modest living and the freedom it offers, as opposed to the endless pursuit of monetary gains. This perspective fosters a sense of wealth in simplicity and financial freedom in the present moment.

- *Relationship Fulfillment:* Many people believe that finding the ideal partner will cure loneliness. However, Stoicism advocates for cultivating self-reliance and inner harmony within yourself. This philosophy suggests building a foundation of self-contentment and emotional independence, creating a healthier and more fulfilling basis for any future relationships.

- *Health and Fitness Goals:* The belief that happiness will come from achieving a specific physical or health goal is common. Stoicism teaches us to appreciate the process of self-care and maintaining health, focusing on the journey and the incremental improvements rather than fixating on an end goal. This approach encourages a more balanced and sustainable lifestyle.

- *Social Recognition:* The quest for fame or social validation as a source of happiness is a trap many fall into. Stoicism, however, proposes cultivating inner virtues such as courage, integrity, and compassion rather than seeking external approval. This mindset encourages a more authentic and fulfilling social existence grounded in true self-worth.

By adopting these Stoic principles, individuals can transform their approach to life, shifting focus from pursuing external validations and achievements to fostering internal contentment and appreciation for the present. This shift enhances personal well-being and leads to a more balanced, fulfilling, and genuinely happy life.

Happiness Through Stoic Practices: Daily Exercises

Negative Visualization

One Stoic practice that bolsters our path to happiness, or eudaimonia, centers on the concept of Negative Visualization. This exercise encourages us to contemplate the impermanence of our lives and the things we hold dear. It might seem counterintuitive to derive happiness from considering potential loss or hardship. However, the Stoics believed that this practice helps to enhance appreciation for what we have now and promotes resilience in the face of adversity.

Visualize, for a moment, how your life would change if you lost something or someone you value. It could be a person, a possession, a job, or even your health. By mentally rehearsing these losses, you start to appreciate their presence in your life more deeply. This exercise isn't intended to foster fear or pessimism. Instead, it helps us cherish our present blessings and prepares us to face potential future challenges with greater stability.

Voluntary Discomfort

Another Stoic exercise conducive to happiness is the practice of Voluntary Discomfort. This practice involves deliberately subjecting ourselves to discomfort or inconvenience. The aim is not to inflict needless suffering but to strengthen our resilience and reduce our dependence on external comforts for our happiness.

Consider implementing small acts of voluntary discomfort in your daily routine. This discomfort could be taking a cold shower, fasting for a day, or sleeping on a hard surface. The idea isn't to punish yourself but to train yourself to be comfortable with discomfort.

The Stoics believed that by regularly experiencing discomfort voluntarily, we become more resilient to involuntary discomfort that life might throw our way. It's a way of immunizing ourselves against future hardships. Furthermore, it helps us appreciate the comforts we often take for granted, enhancing our sense of contentment.

View from Above

The final exercise is a meditative practice known as the View from Above. This practice helps us gain a broader perspective on our lives, enabling us to see our problems, worries, and anxieties in a larger context. It provides us with a valuable reminder of our place in the universe, fostering humility, tranquility, and a sense of interconnectedness.

To practice the View from Above, picture yourself from an external viewpoint, starting from a few feet away and gradually expanding your perspective. Visualize your surroundings: city, country, the Earth, and the vast expanse of the cosmos.

Observe how your problems, which might have seemed overwhelming at first, appear insignificant from this cosmic perspective. This shift in perspective can help us realize that many of the things we worry about are trivial in the grand scheme of things, fostering serenity and freeing us from unnecessary stress and anxiety. Deep visualization is the key to this exercise; use your imagination.

These three Stoic exercises – Negative Visualization, Voluntary Discomfort, and the View from Above – provide practical strategies for cultivating happiness. They encourage us to appreciate what we have, build resilience, gain perspective, and focus on what truly matters. By integrating these practices into our lives, we are taking proactive steps towards achieving eudaimonia, the Stoic ideal of a fulfilled, meaningful life.

So, begin today. Engage with these exercises, reflect on your experiences, and observe the changes in your outlook. Remember, pursuing happiness isn't a search for fleeting pleasures or external validation but a commitment to living by following virtue, wisdom, and our true nature. This is the path to eudaimonia and true, lasting happiness. A path that, with practice and perseverance, we can all tread.

Embrace Simplicity through Stoicism

The philosophy of Stoicism centers on the principle of living simply. This approach involves paring down life's essentials, emphasizing the importance of character and inner resources for happiness.

Seneca, in "Letters from a Stoic," underscores the alignment of goodness with straightforwardness and simplicity. He notes that life's necessities are easily attained, unlike luxuries, which demand significant effort.

Stoicism teaches that a fulfilling life is under our control, mainly through our character. Our ability to find happiness originates from this understanding. Recognizing that true contentment comes from within is crucial.

In "Meditations," Marcus Aurelius remarks that few things are essential for a happy life, all of which are within ourselves. While basic needs are essential, many of us burden our lives with non-essential items—stoicism advocates for eliminating all that is unnecessary, extending beyond physical items to thoughts and actions.

Marcus Aurelius advises in "Meditations" that limiting our redundant words and actions can lead to tranquility and leisure. He encourages continual evaluation of the necessity of our actions and thoughts.

To be mindful, we must assess whether our thoughts and actions are beneficial. Essentials are those that drive progress and enhance happiness and self-improvement. Everything else is surplus. We should consistently evaluate every aspect of our lives – belongings, thoughts, and actions – and remove what is unnecessary.

Consider the scenario of decluttering a home. A common challenge many face is accumulating items that we may need someday. However, these items often become unused, creating space and clutter. Applying Stoic principles, one would examine each item critically, asking if it genuinely contributes to their well-being or merely occupies space. This process declutters the physical space and brings mental clarity as one learns to distinguish between what is truly necessary and what is not.

Furthermore, simplifying life isn't limited to tangible items. It also applies to our commitments and social interactions. For instance, one might have a packed schedule filled with social events, meetings, and activities. Applying Stoic wisdom would evaluate each commitment's value and impact on their overall well-being. If specific engagements or activities are found to be stressful or unfulfilling, it might be wise to reduce or eliminate them. This approach leads to a more focused and meaningful use of time, aligning with the Stoic pursuit of a tranquil and purposeful life.

Simplifying life according to Stoic principles involves a holistic review of one's lifestyle, encompassing both the physical and the psychological, to foster a life focused on essential, fulfilling, and character-building experiences.

FIVE

Building a Grounded Mindset Brick-by-Brick

Imagine you are a surfer riding a massive wave. The wave is powerful, unpredictable, and beyond your control. Yet, you remain balanced, focused, and in control of your actions. You ride the wave, not by trying to control it but by adapting to its movements by responding with agility and composure. This is the essence of resilience, a crucial aspect of Stoic philosophy and the focus of this chapter.

Resilience, in its simplest form, is the ability to bounce back from adversity. It's about facing life's challenges, not with fear or despair, but with courage and a sense of purpose. It's about learning from our experiences, growing stronger with each setback, and moving forward with renewed vigor and resolve. In this chapter, we'll explore the Stoic approach to resilience, focusing on the dichotomy of control, premeditation of adversities, and the cultivation of equanimity.

Stoicism and Mental Toughness: The Dichotomy of Control

Understanding What's in Our Control

Imagine you're in a garden, surrounded by a variety of plants. Some plants are thriving, their leaves lush and vibrant, while others are wilting, their leaves dry and dull. You water the plants, prune them, and ensure they get enough sunlight. Yet, despite your best efforts, you can't control how they grow. You can influence their growth, but you can't control it.

This principle is the essence of the Stoic dichotomy of control. The Stoics believed that some things are within our control, while others are not. Our actions, attitudes, and responses are within our control. But the outcomes of our actions, the actions of others, and the events of the world are not within our control.

This idea might seem obvious, but we often forget this distinction in our daily lives. We stress over things we can't control and neglect the things we can. We blame ourselves for outcomes that are beyond our control and take for granted the choices that are within our control.

Accepting What's Not in Our Control

Accepting what's not in our control is like letting go of the illusion that we can control the waves. It's about acknowledging the unpredictability of life and focusing our efforts on what we can influence rather than what we can't.

This doesn't mean we should be passive or indifferent to the world around us. We can still strive to influence events, to make a positive impact, and to shape our destiny. But we do so with the understanding that the final outcome is not in our hands.

This acceptance is liberating. It frees us from the pressure of unrealistic expectations, the stress of constant worry, and the fear of failure. It allows us to engage fully with the present moment, make the most of our choices, and find peace amidst life's chaos.

Practicing the Dichotomy of Control

Practicing the dichotomy of control is like training yourself to ride the waves. It's a skill that can be cultivated with practice, patience, and persistence.

Here are some practical steps to practice the dichotomy of control:

- Start your day by reminding yourself of the dichotomy of control. Tell yourself: "Today, I will focus on what's within my control and accept what's not."

- When faced with a challenge, ask yourself: "Is this within my control?" If it is, focus on how you can address it. If it's not, accept it as it is and focus on how you can respond to it.

- At the end of the day, reflect on how well you practiced the dichotomy of control. Identify instances where you succeeded and areas where you need improvement.

With regular practice, the dichotomy of control can become second nature, a guiding principle that empowers you to navigate life with resilience and grace. It's a slight shift in mindset that can make a big difference in your life. So, choose to focus on what's within your control and embrace the freedom, the resilience, and the peace that comes with it.

Strategies for Building Resilience: A Stoic Approach

Premeditation of Adversities

Anticipating adversity might seem like a recipe for anxiety, but when practiced mindfully, it can be an effective tool for building resilience. This is the essence of premeditation of adversities, a Stoic practice that involves visualizing potential setbacks and planning ways to cope with them.

This practice is not about dwelling on negatives or expecting the worst. Instead, it provides a mental rehearsal for potential challenges, helping us to cultivate resilience and equip ourselves to handle difficulties with greater stability.

Consider a situation you worry about – a difficult conversation, project deadline, or personal challenge. Visualize the situation in vivid detail. Instead of focusing on what could go wrong, shift your focus to how you would respond to these adversities.

What actions can you take? What resources can you draw upon? How can you uphold your values and maintain your composure, even in the face of adversity? By answering these questions, you prepare yourself for potential challenges and reinforce your resilience and your capacity to bounce back from adversity.

Embracing Obstacles as Opportunities

Life, as we know, is replete with obstacles. While our instinct might be to avoid these obstacles, Stoicism encourages us to embrace them, to see them not as hindrances but as opportunities for growth and learning.

This shift in perspective is at the heart of Stoic resilience. It's about reframing our challenges, viewing them as stepping stones rather than stumbling blocks. It's about finding the silver lining in every situation, the lesson in every setback, and the opportunity in every obstacle.

Next time you encounter an obstacle, pause for a moment. Instead of reacting with frustration or despair, ask yourself... What can I learn from this situation? How can I grow from this experience? How can this obstacle become an opportunity?

By asking these questions, you shift your focus from the obstacle to your response. You empower yourself to transform challenges into opportunities, setbacks into stepping stones, and adversities into adventures.

Cultivating Equanimity

Maintaining a balanced mind can be daunting in the face of life's ups and downs. Yet, this is precisely what the Stoics strived for. They cultivated equanimity, a state of mental calm and composure, regardless of the circumstances.

Equanimity, in the Stoic sense, is not about suppressing emotions or adopting a passive attitude. It's about responding to life's events with understanding and acceptance rather than reacting impulsively. It's about maintaining a steady mind, even in the face of adversity. If the event has already happened, what good is it to react in a way that will only cause more harm? It would help if you had a clear mind to come up with a way forward. Equanimity is commonly found in great decision-makers and negotiators. Being able to control your emotions and think clearly in any situation is a cornerstone of emotional intelligence. Next time you are being pulled into a stressful situation, don't react. Take a step back, breathe, and take a moment to reflect on your emotions before responding.

Equanimity starts with mindfulness – being present in the here and now, observing our thoughts and emotions without judgment. This mindful awareness allows us to respond to events with wisdom and composure rather than reacting impulsively or habitually.

Practices such as meditation, journaling, and mindful breathing can help cultivate equanimity. They provide a space for self-reflection, observing our thoughts and emotions, and developing a balanced, composed mind. There's no single easy way to build stability; it's a way of life and thinking you must commit to. As you become more mindful, you can learn more advanced techniques to calm your mind and develop emotional intelligence.

The path to resilience is not a straight line but a winding road filled with obstacles, opportunities, setbacks, and stepping stones. As we navigate this path, let's keep in mind these Stoic strategies. Let's practice the premeditation of adversities, embrace obstacles as opportunities, and cultivate equanimity. With these strategies in our toolkit, we can build resilience, not just as a temporary trait but as a lifelong strength. We can ride the waves of life, not with fear or despair but with courage, composure, and an unwavering commitment to our Stoic principles.

Stoicism and Resilience: Case Study

James Stockdale: Stoicism in a POW Camp

Meet James Stockdale, a United States Navy vice admiral and aviator who endured a harrowing experience as a prisoner of war (POW) during the Vietnam War. His story is not just a tale of survival but also an inspiring example of how Stoic philosophy can provide strength and resilience in the face of unimaginable hardships.

Stockdale's plane was shot down over North Vietnam on September 9, 1965. Captured soon after, he spent the next seven and a half years in the infamous Hỏa Lò Prison, also known as the "Hanoi Hilton." His time in captivity was marked by brutal treatment and conditions that tested the limits of human endurance.

The physical torture Stockdale endured was extreme. He was routinely beaten, denied medical care, and held in solitary confinement for long periods. The most harrowing experience came when he was tortured for four days straight, an ordeal that left him with a broken leg and dislocated shoulder. Despite the physical agony, Stockdale refused to capitulate to his captors' demands for propaganda statements.

In addition to physical torture, Stockdale and other POWs faced psychological torment. They were subjected to isolation, manipulation, and relentless attempts to break their spirit. Stockdale, however, turned to the teachings of Stoicism, a philosophy he had studied in college, to help him cope.

Zeno of Citium, in Athens, initiated the philosophical school of Stoicism during the early part of the 3rd century BC. It teaches the development of self-control and fortitude as a means of overcoming destructive emotions. Developing clear and impartial thinking skills enables an individual to comprehend the concept of universal reason, known as logos. For Stockdale, these teachings were a lifeline. He embraced the idea that while he could not control his circumstances, he could control his response to them. This belief allowed him to maintain his dignity and resolve despite seemingly insurmountable odds.

Stockdale's commitment to Stoicism was evident in his actions. He created a covert communication system to help the POWs resist their captors and maintain a chain of command. He also inflicted self-harm, cutting his scalp and beating his face to be unrecognizable, thus thwarting his captors' plan to film him in a propaganda video.

The Stoic principle of focusing on what one can control and accepting what one cannot was pivotal for Stockdale. He knew he couldn't control the duration of his imprisonment or the actions of his captors, but he could control his attitude and actions within the prison walls. This mindset was not only crucial for his own survival but also served as an inspiration to his fellow POWs.

Don't get his resolve confused with optimism. In fact, Stockdale observed that there were differences in survival between captives like him who were Stoic (and present-facing) and those who were needlessly optimistic. He describes the difference between Stoics and optimists like this:

[The optimists] were the ones who said, "We're going to be out by Christmas." And Christmas would come, and Christmas would go. Then they'd say, "We're going to be out by Easter." And Easter would come, and Easter would go. And then Thanksgiving, and then it would be Christmas again. And they died of a broken heart. This is a critical lesson. You must never confuse faith that you will prevail in the end—which you can never afford to lose—with the discipline to confront the most brutal facts of your current reality, whatever they might be. (Collins, 2023)

Stockdale's endurance and leadership were recognized after his release in 1973. He received multiple honors, including the Medal of Honor, the United States military's highest decoration. In his later years, he often spoke about the role of Stoicism in his survival, highlighting how the philosophy provided a framework for dealing with adversity.

In conclusion, Stockdale's stoic demeanor was legendary among his fellow prisoners. Despite enduring torture, isolation, and physical degradation, he never broke. Moreover, he provided a source of inspiration for those around him. James Stockdale's experience as a POW is a profound case study of resilience and the power of philosophy in real-life situations. His application of Stoic principles under extreme conditions is a testament to the human spirit's capacity to endure and overcome. Stoicism, with its focus on inner strength, self-control, and the distinction between what we can and cannot control, played an essential role in Stockdale's survival and inspired those facing their battles today.

Building Resilience: Journaling Exercises

In the realm of personal growth and self-improvement, the practice of journaling holds a significant place. More than a mere record of daily events, writing is an empowering tool you can use to reflect. It can help us track our progress, explore our thoughts and emotions, and better understand ourselves and our experiences. In this context, we'll explore how journaling can bolster our resilience, drawing on the principles of Stoicism.

Reflecting on the Dichotomy of Control

The dichotomy of control is a foundational Stoic principle that encourages us to focus on what's in our control and accept what's not. Journaling offers a practical way to explore and apply this principle in our daily lives.

Try this:

1. At the end of each day, take a few moments to reflect on your experiences.
2. Write about the situations you faced, the decisions you made, and the emotions you felt.
3. As you write, identify which aspects of your experiences were within your control and which were not.

For instance, you may write about a difficult conversation you had with a colleague. While you couldn't control your colleague's reactions or responses, you could control your own words, actions, and attitudes. Acknowledging this distinction in your journal can help reinforce the dichotomy of control, guiding your future actions and fostering resilience.

Recording Adversities and Responses

Challenges and setbacks are part and parcel of life. Each adversity we face presents an opportunity to build resilience to bounce back stronger and wiser. Journaling about these adversities and our responses can provide valuable insights into our resilience-building process.

Here's a simple practice: Write about it in your journal whenever you face a challenge or setback. Describe the situation, your initial reactions, and the actions you took. Reflect on how you could apply Stoic principles, such as the dichotomy of control or the view from above, in responding to adversity.

For example, if you faced a job rejection, you could write about how you dealt with the disappointment, how you used the dichotomy of control to focus on improving your skills and seeking other opportunities, and how you viewed the situation from a broader perspective.

By recording adversities and responses in your journal, you turn your challenges into learning opportunities and your setbacks into stepping stones, fostering resilience and personal growth.

Tracking Progress in Resilience

Resilience is not a destination but a journey - a journey marked by growth, learning, and continuous improvement.

Journaling can serve as a roadmap for this journey, helping you track your progress, recognize your growth, and identify areas for further development.

Consider this practice: Review your journal entries regularly and reflect on your progress in

resilience. Look for patterns in your responses to adversities, note the application of Stoic principles, and acknowledge the growth in your resilience.

For example, over time, you're better able to manage disappointment, more consistent in applying the dichotomy of control, or more composed in the face of challenges. Recognizing these signs of progress can boost your motivation, reinforce your commitment to resilience, and inspire you to continue your journey with renewed vigor and enthusiasm.

As you venture forth on your path to resilience, remember that every step, every stumble, every leap is a part of the process. Embrace the journey with openness, patience, and perseverance. Use the tools of Stoicism and journaling to navigate the path, to learn, to grow, and to build resilience. And as you do, know that with each word you write, each reflection you make, and each insight you gain, you're not just becoming more resilient; you're becoming more you - a stronger, wiser, more resilient you. And that, in itself, is a journey worth undertaking.

Now, as we prepare to explore the next chapter of our Stoic exploration, remember the words of Seneca,

> "A gem cannot be polished without friction, nor a man perfected without trials."

With resilience as our gem and Stoicism as our polisher, let's continue our journey, ready to face our trials, eager to polish our gem, and committed to perfecting our true selves.

SIX

Accepting The Uncontrollable

Imagine looking over at the vast ocean, watching the waves rise and fall. They are powerful, relentless, and beyond your control. Yet, something is awe-inspiring about them, something that fills you with a sense of peace and acceptance. This is what acceptance in Stoicism feels like. It's about acknowledging the waves of life—the things we cannot control—and finding peace, not in trying to control them, but in learning to ride them.

The Art of Acceptance

Amor Fati: Love of Fate

The Stoic concept of acceptance is encapsulated in the Latin phrase "Amor Fati," which translates to "love of fate." This concept is not a passive acceptance or a resigned surrender but an active, joyful embrace of whatever life brings our way.

Consider a farmer planting seeds in a field. The farmer does his part - he tills the soil, sows the seeds, waters the plants. But he cannot control the weather, the sunlight, or the growth of the seeds. He accepts these factors, knowing they are beyond his control. He does his part and accepts whatever outcome nature brings. In essence, it is Amor Fati - doing our part and loving whatever fate brings our way.

Acceptance of Death and Impermanence

Another crucial aspect of Stoic acceptance is the acknowledgment of death and impermanence. For the Stoics, death was not something to be feared or avoided but simply a natural part of life. By accepting death, we free ourselves from the fear of the unknown, enabling us to live more fully and authentically.

Imagine watching a sunset. The beauty of the sunset lies in its transience, in the fleeting interplay of light and color. We don't mourn the day's passing; we appreciate the sunset for what it is - a transient display of nature's beauty. Similarly, by accepting the impermanence of life, we can enjoy each moment more deeply, living our lives like a beautiful sunset - transient yet fulfilling.

Embracing the Natural Order of the Universe

Stoic acceptance also involves embracing the natural order of the universe. The Stoics believed that the universe revolves around a rational principle called the Logos. By accepting and aligning ourselves with this natural order, we can live in harmony with the universe, finding peace amidst the chaos of life.

Imagine a tree standing tall in a forest. The tree doesn't resist the changing seasons, the falling leaves, or the howling winds. It stands tall, firmly rooted, accepting whatever nature brings its way. It grows at its own pace, in its own time, in accordance with the natural order. As we navigate the forests of our lives, we can learn from the tree, standing tall amidst the changes, growing in harmony with the natural order.

The waves will rise and fall in this vast, unpredictable ocean of life. But as we embrace the Stoic art of acceptance, we learn to ride these waves with grace and composure. We learn to love our fate, accept death and impermanence, and embrace the universe's natural order. And as we do, we find an inner peace that is as vast and deep as the ocean.

So, as you navigate the waves of life, remember the words of Marcus Aurelius:

> "Accept whatever comes to you woven in the pattern of your destiny, for what could more aptly fit your needs?"

With these words as our guiding principle, let's continue to explore the depths of Stoicism, diving deeper into the art of acceptance and emerging stronger, wiser, and more resilient.

Techniques for Practicing Acceptance: Stoic Strategies

Contemplation of the Sage

In the realm of Stoicism, the figure of the 'Sage' holds a significant place. The Sage is the embodiment of Stoic wisdom, a paragon of virtue, an ideal that we strive to emulate. The Sage responds to all favorable or unfavorable events with calmness and acceptance. This stoic acceptance is not a passive resignation but an active affirmation of life in all its complexity.

The technique of Contemplation of the Sage is a powerful tool for practicing acceptance. It involves visualizing how a Sage would respond to various life situations. By pondering this, we can gain insights into accepting life's events with grace and serenity.

Imagine you're facing a difficult situation, perhaps a setback at work or a conflict in a relationship. Pause momentarily and visualize how a Sage would respond to this situation. What actions would they take? What attitudes would they adopt? How would they maintain their composure and acceptance, even in the face of adversity?

By contemplating the Sage, we create a mental model of stoic acceptance. This model serves as a guide, helping us navigate life's challenges with equanimity and acceptance. It's like having a compass that always points towards acceptance, no matter how stormy the seas of life may get.

Practicing Detachment

Another effective strategy for cultivating acceptance is the practice of detachment. Detachment, in the Stoic sense, is not about isolating ourselves or suppressing our emotions. It's about developing a balanced perspective, where we're engaged with life but not entangled in it.

Detachment involves observing our experiences without getting swept up in them. It's about allowing life's events to unfold without clinging to them or resisting them. It's about experiencing our emotions without becoming overwhelmed by them.

Practicing detachment can be as simple as setting aside a few moments each day to observe our thoughts and feelings. As we observe them, we can remind ourselves that we are not our thoughts or feelings. They are part of our experience, but they do not define us. By cultivating this sense of detachment, we can experience life more fully, respond to events more effectively, and accept whatever comes our way with poise and grace.

Acceptance Meditation

Meditation is a powerful tool for building acceptance. It allows us to quiet the mind, observe our thoughts and feelings, and develop a more profound sense of tranquility.

To practice acceptance meditation:

1. Find a quiet spot and sit comfortably.
2. Close your eyes and take a few deep breaths.
3. Allow your body and mind to relax.
4. Turn your attention to your breath, observing its rhythm, rise, and fall without trying to change or control it.

As you meditate, your thoughts and feelings will start to come up. Instead of engaging with them or resisting them, simply observe them. Watch them come and go like clouds passing in the sky. If you find yourself getting caught up in a thought or feeling, gently bring your focus back to your breath.

Through this practice, you cultivate an attitude of non-judgmental observation of acceptance towards your thoughts and feelings. You realize that you can experience them without being controlled by them. You learn to ride the waves of your mind with balance and stability, accepting whatever arises with grace and serenity.

As you explore these techniques - Contemplation of the Sage, practicing detachment, and acceptance meditation - remember that acceptance is not a destination but a practice. It's an ongoing process of embracing life in all its complexity, of riding its waves with balance and grace. So, keep practicing, keep exploring, and keep accepting. With each step, you're not just becoming more accepting; you're becoming more resilient, balanced, and at peace. And isn't that what we all strive for?

Stoicism and Acceptance: Case Study

Viktor Frankl, an Austrian neurologist, psychiatrist, and Holocaust survivor, stands as a profound example of Stoicism in the face of unimaginable adversity. Born in Vienna in 1905, Frankl founded logotherapy, a form of existential analysis. His experiences during the Holocaust profoundly shaped his philosophical and professional outlook, particularly his views on the human ability to be resilient and find meaning in suffering.

Frankl was arrested in 1942 along with his wife, parents, and brother, and they were transported to the Theresienstadt ghetto. His father died there of starvation and pneumonia. In 1944, Frankl and his remaining family were sent to Auschwitz, where his mother and brother were killed. His wife, Tilly, was transferred to another camp and died shortly before the war ended. During his time in Auschwitz and later in Kaufering and Türkheim (subsidiary camps of Dachau), Frankl labored under extreme conditions, enduring starvation, brutality, and constant dehumanization.

Despite these harrowing experiences, Frankl managed to find moments of psychological relief by fixating on the thoughts of his wife and his desire to rewrite the manuscript of his book, which had been confiscated in Auschwitz. His ability to maintain a sense of purpose and inner freedom in the face of physical suffering is a testament to his stoic attitude. Frankl often reflected on Nietzsche's words: "He who has a why to live for can bear almost any how," which became a central tenet in his psychological theory.

Frankl's Stoicism is particularly evident in his theory of logotherapy, which he developed further after his liberation from the concentration camps in 1945. Logotherapy posits that the primary motivational force in humans is to find meaning in life. Frankl believed that even in the most savage and dehumanizing situations, life can still have meaning and that suffering itself can be a source of meaning. He argued that individuals could find meaning through experiencing something (like love), through creating a work or doing a deed, and most importantly, through the attitude one takes toward unavoidable suffering.

His most famous work, "Man's Search for Meaning," written in nine days following his release, details his experiences in the concentration camps and presents his ideas of logotherapy. In this book, Frankl narrates how he and other inmates found meaning in their suffering, which provided them with the will to endure the horrors of camp life. He emphasized the importance of hope, the freedom to choose one's attitude at all times, and the personal responsibility to find meaning in life, regardless of external conditions.

Frankl's Stoicism is seen in his endurance of the horrors of the Holocaust and in his ability to maintain a sense of purpose and inner dignity despite the external chaos and cruelty. He believed that even in the most despairing of circumstances, a person could exercise the freedom to choose their attitude and find meaning in their suffering. This belief was not just a theoretical proposition but a lived reality for Frankl, who practiced this stoic principle throughout his ordeal in the concentration camps.

In conclusion, Viktor Frankl's life and work offer a powerful illustration of Stoicism in action. His experiences during the Holocaust, where he faced and accepted the uncontrollable with remarkable resilience, and his subsequent development of logotherapy underscore the stoic belief in the power of the human spirit to find meaning and purpose in life, even in the face of the most severe adversity. His legacy is a testament to the strength of the human will and the enduring capacity to find hope and meaning in life, no matter the circumstances.

Reflective Prompts for Acceptance: Journaling Exercises

Reflecting on Amor Fati

The first exercise invites you to reflect on Amor Fati, the Stoic practice of loving one's fate. Grab your journal and think about a recent event in your life that was challenging or did not pan out the way you desired. It may be a personal setback, a professional disappointment, or an unexpected change.

Instead of dwelling on this event's negative aspects, try reframing your perspective. Write about how you can interpret this event as a part of your unique life script that had to happen in that exact way. Consider how this event, although seemingly unfavorable, could contribute to your personal growth or lead to new opportunities. What lessons have you learned? How have you grown? How will you continue to grow?

Journaling about Death and Impermanence

The second exercise encourages you to contemplate death and impermanence, two central themes of Stoic philosophy. Think about how the recognition of life's fleeting nature affects your perspective. Does it make your problems seem smaller? Does it encourage you to live more fully and authentically? Reflect on these questions and pen down your thoughts.

Remember, this is not intended to be a morbid exercise but rather a way to bring clarity to your life. Through contemplating death and impermanence, we can learn to appreciate life more deeply, to focus on what truly matters, and to let go of trivial concerns.

Take a mental note of Instances of Acceptance.

In the final exercise, recall the moments where you have practiced acceptance. If you haven't, think of a past setback you haven't let go of and are finally ready to accept. It could be accepting a situation you cannot change, an outcome you did not desire, or even accepting yourself, complete with all your strengths and weaknesses.

As you remember these instances, pay attention to how accepting feels. Is there a sense of relief? A sense of peace? Do you feel lighter, freer, or more at ease? Notice these feelings and reflect on them in your journal.

Practicing acceptance can lead to a profound shift in how we experience life. It can free us from the need to control everything, allowing us to find peace in the present moment. And it can help us build resilience, stability, and a deep sense of contentment.

These journaling exercises, while simple, can profoundly impact your understanding and practice of Stoicism. They offer a practical way to engage with Stoic principles, to reflect on your experiences, and to integrate Stoic wisdom into your daily life.

Stoicism, at its core, is about wisdom, courage, justice, and temperance. It's about understanding the nature of the universe, our place in it, and how to live in harmony with it. It's about cultivating virtue, managing our emotions, and leading a fulfilling life.

Stoicism is not just a philosophy; it's a way of life. A path that, with practice, we can all tread. So, as we continue our exploration of Stoicism, let's keep these points in mind. Let's strive to understand, practice, and live Stoicism to the best of our ability.

As we conclude this chapter, let's carry forward this spirit of acceptance, this commitment to Stoic principles, and this dedication to personal growth. As we turn the page, let's prepare ourselves for the next phase of our exploration, where we will delve into the role of Stoicism in building confidence and navigating the intricacies of our modern world.

SEVEN

Unlock Unshakable Confidence

When we think of confidence, images of assertive speakers, fearless leaders, or triumphant athletes may come to mind. However, Stoicism offers a different perspective on confidence, one that transcends public speaking prowess or physical strength. In the Stoic view, confidence is an inner strength, a steadfast belief in one's virtues, wisdom, and self-sufficiency.

Confidence Through Stoic Eyes

Confidence in Virtue

The Stoics held virtue in high regard, considering it the highest good and the foundation of a fulfilling life. But how does virtue relate to confidence? The answer lies in the inherent worth of virtue. When we cultivate virtues like wisdom, courage, justice, and temperance, we build a solid moral foundation for our lives. This moral foundation breeds confidence – not a fleeting, situational confidence, but a deep-rooted, unshakeable confidence that comes from living by our values and principles.

Take the virtue of courage, for example. Each time you face a fear, stand up for what is right, or persevere through a challenge, you exercise courage. This repeated practice of courage strengthens your moral fiber and builds your confidence. It's like a muscle that grows stronger with each workout. You come to trust your ability to face adversity, not because you are immune to fear, but because you have the moral courage to face it.

Confidence in Wisdom

Wisdom, another cardinal virtue in Stoicism, is vital in cultivating

- confidence. Stoic wisdom involves:
- Understanding the nature of things.
- Discerning what is within our control and what is not.
- Making informed, rational decisions.

It's about navigating life with discernment, clarity, and a deep understanding of our values and principles. Imagine you're in a maze, trying to find your way out. Wisdom is like a map that guides you through the twists and turns and helps you make informed decisions at each junction. The more you trust this map and successfully navigate the maze, the more your confidence grows. You become confident not because you know the maze inside out but because you trust your wisdom to guide you through it.

Confidence in Self-Sufficiency

The Stoics believed in the importance of self-sufficiency, being content with what we have, and not being overly reliant on external circumstances for our happiness. This sense of self-sufficiency is a powerful source of confidence.

Consider a tree in a forest. The tree is self-sufficient. It draws nutrients from the soil, absorbs sunlight for photosynthesis, and relies on rain for water. It doesn't need to be constantly tended to or cared for. This self-sufficiency gives the tree a kind of confidence. It stands tall and secure in its ability to survive and thrive, regardless of the changing seasons or the other trees in the forest.

We build confidence when we cultivate self-sufficiency, learn to meet our needs, manage our emotions, and find contentment within ourselves. We become like the tree, standing tall amidst life's challenges, secure in our ability to survive and thrive.

As you can see, Stoic confidence is about more than just feeling good about ourselves or projecting a confident image. It's about building inner strength by cultivating virtue, wisdom, and self-sufficiency. It's a confidence that is grounded, authentic, and resilient, capable of weathering the storms of life. That is the confidence that Stoicism helps us cultivate.

Building Confidence: Stoic Techniques and Practices

Practicing Virtue

In the context of Stoicism, virtues represent the highest form of goodness, and their consistent practice is vital to a fulfilling life. By intentionally practicing virtues such as wisdom, courage, justice, and temperance, we build a solid internal foundation that inspires confidence.

How do we actively practice virtue? Begin by identifying a virtue you want to cultivate. Let's say you choose courage. Start by recognizing opportunities in your daily life to demonstrate courage. It can be as small as speaking up in a meeting, expressing a dissenting opinion, or admitting a mistake. The aim is to create a mindset that actively seeks opportunities to practice your chosen virtue.

Remember, practicing virtue is not about grand gestures or significant life changes. It's about small, consistent actions that, over time, become a deeply ingrained part of our character. It's about aligning our daily actions with our highest values, thereby nurturing a strong sense of self-assurance.

Cultivating Wisdom

To the Stoics, wisdom is more than simply accumulated knowledge. It signifies the ability to discern what is truly important in life, make reasoned decisions, and act according to our core values and principles. Cultivating wisdom, therefore, is an essential step towards building Stoic confidence.

Cultivating wisdom involves introspection and continual learning. We can foster wisdom by reflecting on our experiences, learning from our mistakes, and seeking knowledge from various sources. Reading widely, seeking diverse perspectives, and being curious about the world can contribute to our wisdom.

Another way to cultivate wisdom is through meditation and mindfulness. By bringing a mindful awareness to our thoughts and actions, we can gain insights into our habitual patterns, make more conscious choices, and navigate life with greater clarity and confidence.

Embracing Self-Sufficiency

In Stoic philosophy, self-sufficiency doesn't necessarily mean living in isolation or being materially independent. Instead, it's about deriving our sense of worth from within and being content with what we have. It's about recognizing that our happiness and self-esteem depend not on external factors but on our virtues and actions.

To embrace self-sufficiency, we must examine our dependencies, be they material, emotional, or social. Are we overly reliant on our possessions, validation from others, or social status for our self-worth? If so, it's time to shift our focus inward and start deriving our confidence from our virtues, wisdom, and actions.

Practicing gratitude can also enhance our sense of self-sufficiency. By appreciating what we have, we can reduce our dependence on external factors for our happiness and boost our confidence.

Building confidence, the Stoic way, involves a conscientious application of Stoic principles to our daily lives. It's about practicing virtue, cultivating wisdom, and embracing self-sufficiency. As we integrate these practices into our lives, we nurture a grounded, authentic, and resilient form of confidence that stems from our character, values, and inner strength. A confidence that can weather the storms of life and guide us towards a fulfilling, meaningful life.

Stoicism and Confidence: Case Study

Cato the Younger: Confidence in Opposition

Cato the Younger, a steadfast Roman statesman, military leader, and stoic philosopher, is often remembered for his unshakable confidence and unwavering principles during a time of political chaos in the late Roman Republic. Born in 95 BC into a family renowned for its virtue and military prowess, Cato was a descendant of Cato the Elder, a famed Roman senator.

From an early age, Cato was steeped in the stoic philosophy, which would profoundly influence his life and political career. He was known for his austere lifestyle, unyielding moral integrity, and his staunch opposition to the erosion of the Roman Republic's traditions and values. Cato's life was marked by a series of challenges and political battles, most notably against Julius Caesar, whom he viewed as a threat to the Republic's stability and the rule of law.

His tenure marked Cato's early political career as a quaestor, where he was responsible for the state's treasury and finances. He quickly gained a reputation for his incorruptibility and efficiency. As a senator, Cato was a vocal critic of political corruption and the concentration of power in the hands of a few. His steadfast commitment to the Republic's traditional values often put him at odds with more progressive and populist figures, including Julius Caesar.

One of Cato's most significant challenges came during the Catiline Conspiracy in 63 BC, where he played a pivotal role in exposing and suppressing the plot led by Lucius Sergius Catilina to overthrow the Republic. Cato's firm stance and persuasive oratory in the Senate were crucial in mobilizing support against the conspirators, showcasing his unshakable confidence and dedication to the Republic.

Cato's rivalry with Julius Caesar was a defining aspect of his career. He opposed Caesar's quest for military and political power, perceiving it as a direct threat to the Republic's foundations. Cato's opposition to Caesar's consulship, and later to his prolonged command in Gaul, symbolized his commitment to the Republic's constitutional norms and his fear of autocracy.

Cato's Stoicism was most evident during the Civil War between Caesar and Pompey. Cato allied with Pompey, not out of personal loyalty but because he saw Pompey as the Republic's last hope against Caesar's tyranny. After Pompey's defeat at Pharsalus in 48 BC, Cato took charge of the remnants of the senatorial army and retreated to Africa to continue the resistance. His leadership during this turbulent period was marked by the same stoic resilience and unyielding resolve that had characterized his entire life.

The end of Cato's life is the most telling example of his stoic beliefs. Following the defeat at the Battle of Thapsus in 46 BC, Cato chose to take his own life rather than surrender to Caesar. His death was seen not as an act of despair but as a final act of defiance and an assertion of personal freedom and dignity. Cato's suicide was consistent with stoic values, which held that it was better to die with honor than live in dishonor.

Cato's unshakable confidence and Stoicism played a significant role in his journey. He lived his life according to strict moral and ethical principles, undeterred by personal risk or political pressures. His Stoicism was not just a philosophical belief but a practical guide that informed his decisions and actions. He believed in the stoic ideals of virtue, self-control, and rationality, and these principles were reflected in his unwavering commitment to the Republic and its values.

In conclusion, Cato the Younger's life is a testament to the strength of character and the unshakable confidence that Stoicism can engender. His unwavering commitment to the principles of the Roman Republic, his opposition to the concentration of power, and his personal integrity in the face of adversity set him apart as one of the most steadfast defenders of the Roman Republic. Cato's life and tragic end illustrate the stoic belief in the supremacy of virtue and the individual's power to maintain integrity and personal freedom, even in the face of overwhelming challenges.

Confidence Boosters: Journaling Exercises

Reflecting on Virtue

Virtues are like the compass points guiding our actions, decisions, and responses. Embodying these virtues - wisdom, courage, justice, and temperance - can strengthen our character and boost our confidence. Let's engage with a simple yet powerful writing exercise to deepen this connection.

In your journal, choose a virtue that you wish to cultivate. Let's say you choose justice. Think about a situation in your daily life where you can practice this virtue. It could be a situation at work, home, or community. Write about this situation in detail, describing how you can apply the virtue of justice to it.

Justice can involve treating everyone fairly in a group project, standing up against bias or discrimination, or making decisions that consider the welfare of everyone involved. As you write, focus on the steps you can take, the decisions you can make, and the attitudes you can adopt to practice this virtue.

By reflecting on virtue in this way, you gain a deeper understanding of it and create a roadmap for practicing it in your daily life. This practice can strengthen your moral compass, enhance your character, and boost your confidence.

Journaling about Wisdom

Wisdom is the ability to discern what is truly important, make reasoned decisions, and act according to our core values. Journaling provides an excellent platform to explore, cultivate, and apply wisdom in our lives.

In your journal, think about a challenge or decision you're currently facing. Describe the situation in detail, including your options, potential outcomes, and values or principles at stake.

Now, apply the lens of wisdom to this situation. What is the wise course of action? What decision aligns with your values and principles? What potential outcomes should you be prepared for? Write about these reflections in your journal.

By journaling about wisdom in this way, you gain clarity about your situation and practice making reasoned, value-based decisions. This practice can enhance your knowledge, improve your decision-making, and boost your confidence.

Recording Acts of Self-Sufficiency

In Stoic terms, self-sufficiency is about deriving our sense of worth from within and being content with what we have. It's about recognizing that our happiness and self-esteem depend not on external factors but on our virtues and actions.

This writing exercise revolves around capturing moments of self-sufficiency in your daily life. In your journal, record instances where you demonstrated self-sufficiency. It could involve solving a problem on your own, meeting your own emotional needs, or finding contentment in a simple pleasure.

As you record these instances, reflect on how they made you feel. Did you feel empowered? Content? Grateful? Write about these feelings in your journal.

Recording acts of self-sufficiency provides a record of your accomplishments and reinforces your belief in your abilities. This practice can enhance your self-sufficiency, deepen your self-belief, and boost your confidence.

These writing exercises offer a practical way to engage with Stoic principles and cultivate Stoic confidence. They provide a space for reflection, exploration, and self-expression, helping you integrate Stoic wisdom into your daily life. Remember, confidence is not a trait we're born with. It's a skill we can cultivate, a muscle we can strengthen, a light we can kindle within us. And with each word you write, the reflection you make, and the insight you gain, you're igniting that light, strengthening that muscle, cultivating that skill. You're building your Stoic confidence, one word, one reflection, one insight at a time.

Let these exercises guide you as we leave this exploration of Stoic confidence. Let them inspire you to practice virtue, cultivate wisdom, embrace self-sufficiency, and kindle your inner light of confidence. Keep this light burning bright as we step into the next chapter of our exploration, where we will delve into the role of Stoicism in mastering the modern day hustle.

EIGHT

Mastering the Modern-Day Hustle

Picture yourself caught in the hustle and bustle of a busy marketplace. The air is filled with the chatter of negotiations, goods exchange, and coins clink. You are a merchant navigating your way through the crowd, negotiating deals, managing your stall, and dealing with all sorts of unexpected situations. The marketplace is chaotic, unpredictable, and often stressful. Yet, amid this chaos, you find a sense of calm, a sense of control, a sense of fulfillment. This is the promise of Stoicism in the context of work and career.

Much like the bustling marketplace, the modern workplace is rife with challenges and uncertainties. We grapple with difficult decisions, demanding tasks, and the constant pressure to perform. Yet, Stoicism equips us with the mindset and tools to navigate these challenges with resilience, tranquility, and deep-seated confidence. Let's explore how the Stoic principles of the dichotomy of control, virtue ethics, and resilience can guide us in our work and careers.

The Stoic Approach to Work and Career

The dichotomy of Control in Career Decisions

Think about a recent decision you had to make at work. Perhaps it was a negotiation strategy, a choice between two projects, or a response to critical feedback. Now, consider the elements that were within your control - your preparation, your actions, your reactions - and those that were not - the outcome of the negotiation, the response of your boss, and the market conditions.

The Stoic principle of the dichotomy of control teaches us to focus our energy on what's within our control and accept what's not. In the context of career decisions, this means focusing on our actions, efforts, and attitudes while accepting the outcomes, which are often influenced by external factors beyond our control.

Implementing this principle in our work life can liberate us from unnecessary stress and disappointment. It empowers us to make proactive choices and to respond to outcomes with calmness and resilience. It cultivates a sense of inner confidence that stems not from the outcomes we achieve but from the actions we take and the values we uphold.

Virtue Ethics in Professional Life

Stoicism strongly emphasizes virtue ethics, which involves living in accordance with virtues like wisdom, courage, justice, and temperance. These virtues translate into qualities like sound judgment, integrity, fairness, and balance in our professional lives.

Imagine you're leading a team project. Practicing virtue ethics in this context could involve:

- Making decisions that benefit the entire team (wisdom).
- Standing up for a team member who's being treated unfairly (courage).
- Ensuring the workload is distributed equitably (justice).
- Managing your time effectively to avoid burnout (temperance).

By embodying these virtues in our work, we contribute positively to our workplace and derive a deep sense of fulfillment and self-worth. We build a reputation for integrity and credibility, which can open doors to new opportunities and professional growth. And most importantly, we align our work with our values, creating a meaningful career that reflects who we are and what we stand for.

Stoic Resilience in Career Progression

The path to career success is always filled with setbacks, failures, and disappointments. However, Stoicism teaches us to view these not as obstacles but as an opportunity for growth and learning. This is where the Stoic concept of resilience comes into play. Resilience, in the Stoic sense, is not about avoiding setbacks but about learning to bounce back from them. It's about viewing failures as feedback, setbacks as stepping stones, and challenges as opportunities for growth.

Imagine you've just lost a significant client. A Stoic approach to this setback would involve:

- Accepting the loss (dichotomy of control).
- Learning from the experience (wisdom).
- Treating all parties involved with respect (justice).
- Maintaining a balanced perspective (temperance).

By cultivating resilience, we equip ourselves to navigate the ups and downs of our career journey with grace and composure. We learn to adapt to change, grow from adversity, and persist in facing obstacles. And in doing so, we build a career that is fulfilling, meaningful, and aligned with our deepest values.

In the bustling marketplace of the modern workplace, Stoicism serves as our compass, guiding us through the chaos with wisdom, virtue, and resilience. It teaches us to focus on what's within our control, to uphold our values, and to bounce back from setbacks. It equips us to build a successful career and a fulfilling life. In doing so, Stoicism transforms the marketplace from a place of chaos and stress into a place of growth, fulfillment, and profound confidence.

Practical Stoic Techniques for the Workplace

View from Above for Workplace Perspective

In the midst of a challenging work situation, it's easy to lose perspective. Minor setbacks can seem like major disasters, and everyday stresses can feel overwhelming. The Stoic technique, the View from Above, can help us regain perspective and reduce work-related stress.

The View from Above involves visualizing yourself from an external viewpoint and gradually expanding your perspective to encompass a broader view of your situation in a workplace setting; this could mean viewing your current situation in the context of your entire career, your organization's history, or even the larger industry landscape.

For instance, if you're dealing with a project failure, using the View from Above technique, you would first acknowledge the setback, then consider it in the context of all the projects you've handled over your career, then in relation to your organization's achievements and challenges, and finally, in the grand scheme of the industry's successes and failures.

This shift in perspective can help you realize that this setback is but a small bump in the larger journey. It can help us ease the stress and anxiety that often accompany such situations, allowing you to approach your work with a renewed sense of calm and clarity.

Premeditation Malorum for Handling Work Challenges

Workplace challenges are inevitable. Whether it's meeting a tight deadline, dealing with a difficult colleague, or navigating a career transition, these challenges can often cause stress and anxiety. The Stoic practice of Premeditatio Malorum, or premeditation of evils, can equip us with the mindset to handle work challenges more effectively.

Premeditatio Malorum involves visualizing potential challenges or adversities and contemplating how you would handle them. This practice prepares you mentally and emotionally for the challenge, reducing anxiety and enhancing your problem-solving abilities.

For example, if you're about to have a difficult conversation with a colleague, you could practice Premeditatio Malorum by visualizing how the conversation might go, anticipating possible reactions, and planning your responses. This preparation can help you approach the conversation with more confidence and composure and lead to a more constructive outcome.

The Dichotomy of Control

The Dichotomy of Control, a fundamental concept in Stoic philosophy, teaches the importance of distinguishing between what we can control and what we cannot. In today's fast-paced and highly competitive career landscape, this principle offers a powerful tool for personal and professional development.

Firstly, grasping and embracing the concept of the Dichotomy of Control can lead to a marked decrease in stress and anxiety, which are often prevalent in today's work environments. We can direct our energy more productively by focusing on aspects of our careers that are within our control – such as our skills, attitudes, and efforts. This mindset encourages a proactive approach to career advancement, where one is more inclined to seek out opportunities for learning and self-improvement rather than being paralyzed by the fear of failure or external factors beyond one's control.

Moreover, this philosophy aids in setting realistic goals and expectations. In a world where external success markers often dominate career narratives, the Dichotomy of Control reminds us to value internal growth and personal achievements. For example, individuals can focus on developing competencies and acquiring new skills rather than fixating on a specific job title or salary, which external factors like market demand or company policies may influence. This shift in perspective fosters a sense of fulfillment and motivation, irrespective of external validations.

Additionally, the Dichotomy of Control cultivates resilience, a crucial trait in today's ever-evolving job market. By acknowledging that certain events – such as organizational changes, economic downturns, or even global pandemics – are outside our control, we can better adapt to these challenges. Instead of dwelling on the unpredictability and unfairness of these situations, we can concentrate on adapting our strategies, learning from the experience, and moving forward.

Furthermore, this approach enhances decision-making and prioritization skills. We become more strategic in our actions by constantly assessing what aspects of a situation we can influence. It means investing time and resources in initiatives that are likely to yield results rather than wasting effort on unchangeable circumstances.

Applying the Dichotomy of Control in career advancement in today's world empowers individuals to navigate the complexities of the modern workplace with greater composure, clarity, and purpose. It encourages a focus on personal growth and resilience, leading to a more fulfilling and sustainable career path.

Incorporating these Stoic techniques into your work life can seriously improve your ability to manage stress, maintain perspective, and handle challenges. They provide practical tools for cultivating a mindset of resilience, stability, and confidence, enabling you to navigate your work life with greater ease and effectiveness. These practices can serve as your compass, guiding you through the bustling marketplace of the modern workplace helping you survive and thrive.

Stoicism in The Modern Day: Case Study One

Elon Musk was born in South Africa. He is a figure who epitomizes the intersection of visionary innovation and Stoic resilience. His journey from an intelligent but often isolated child in South Africa to one of the most influential entrepreneurs of the 21st century reflects many Stoic virtues, particularly in his approach to challenges, failures, and his vision for the future.

Musk's early life was not easy. Bullied in school and dealing with a complex family situation, he turned to books and computers as an escape. He taught himself programming and, at the age of 12, sold a video game he created called Blastar. This early display of initiative and self-reliance echoes the Stoic principle of focusing on one's own actions and development.

In 1995, Musk dropped out of a PhD program at Stanford University to pursue entrepreneurial aspirations in the burgeoning field of the internet. He was a co-founder of Zip2, which offered maps and business directories for newspaper clients. Despite the challenges of launching a startup, Musk's persistence paid off when Compaq acquired Zip2 for almost $300 million in 1999. This early success, however, did not come without struggles and setbacks, which Musk faced with a Stoic-like resilience.

Stoicism teaches the importance of enduring hardships and viewing obstacles as opportunities for growth – a theme evident in Musk's career. After Zip2, he founded X.com, which eventually became PayPal. Despite facing skepticism and operational challenges, Musk remained steadfast, a characteristic that paid off when eBay bought PayPal for $1.5 billion in 2002.

Perhaps the most striking examples of Musk's application of Stoic virtues are found in his ventures with SpaceX and Tesla. When he started SpaceX in 2002, his goal was to make space exploration more affordable. The early years were fraught with many failures; even the first three launches of the Falcon 1 rocket failed. Despite these setbacks, Musk persisted, embodying the Stoic principle of focusing on what he could control - his effort and determination. His perseverance was rewarded when the fourth launch of Falcon 1 in 2008 was successful, leading to a significant contract with NASA.

Tesla Motors, which Musk co-founded, also faced significant challenges. The automotive industry was skeptical of electric cars, and Tesla struggled with production issues and financial constraints. Yet, Musk's Stoic-like focus on his vision and his ability to stay the course during difficult times was pivotal in Tesla becoming a leader in electric vehicles.

Musk's approach to risk also reflects Stoic principles. Stoicism teaches the acceptance of failure as a part of life and the importance of pursuing one's values despite potential setbacks. Musk invested his own fortune into his ventures, showing a willingness to risk personal loss for a greater goal, a distinctly Stoic trait.

In addition to these ventures, Musk's involvement in projects like Neuralink and The Boring Company further demonstrates his Stoic-like approach to life and business. He tackles problems that he believes are critical to humanity's future, showing a focus on rational action and the common good, consistent with Stoic ethics.

Furthermore, Musk's public persona and approach to criticism and stress reflect Stoic influences. He often discusses the importance of reasoning, self-discipline, and mental fortitude, which are critical aspects of Stoic philosophy.

In conclusion, Elon Musk's journey, marked by his ability to face adversity, stay focused on long-term goals, and be resilient in the face of adversity, aligns closely with the teachings of Stoicism. His life demonstrates the Stoic virtues of courage, perseverance, rationality, and a commitment to the greater good. His story is a testament to the enduring relevance of Stoic principles in navigating the complexities and challenges of modern entrepreneurial endeavors.

Stoicism in The Modern Day: Case Study Two

Theodore Roosevelt, the 26th President of the United States, remains a resounding example of stoic resilience, overcoming numerous hardships while achieving remarkable success. His life, marked by both personal tragedy and physical ailments, stands as a testament to the power of stoic principles in the face of adversity.

Born into the world on October 27, 1858, in the bustling metropolis of New York City, Roosevelt faced his first challenge early in life: a debilitating asthma condition. Despite this, he adopted a strenuous lifestyle, a direct embodiment of his later maxim, "The Strenuous Life," which advocated for facing challenges head-on. This approach was not only a remedy for his physical health but also a cornerstone of his mental resilience.

Roosevelt's life was marked by poignant tragedy. In 1884, he endured a devastating double loss: his mother, Martha Bulloch

Roosevelt, and his first wife, Alice Hathaway Lee, died on the same day, February 14, in the same house. Roosevelt's diary entry for that day was a single, sorrowful 'X,' underlining the immense grief that he experienced.

Undeterred by personal loss, Roosevelt's political career flourished. He served as a New York State Assemblyman, a U.S. Civil Service Commissioner, the President of the New York City Police Board, and the Assistant Secretary of the Navy. During the Spanish-American War, he led the Rough Riders, a volunteer cavalry unit, in a famous charge up San Juan Hill, exemplifying his courage and leadership.

In 1901, following the tragic assassination of President William McKinley, Theodore Roosevelt, who was serving as Vice President at the time, ascended to the Presidency. His tenure was marked by progressive policies, including the conservation of natural resources, the regulation of monopolies, and the negotiation of the Panama Canal Treaty. Theodore was awarded the Nobel Peace Prize in 1906, a recognition for his successful mediation in the Russo-Japanese War, setting a precedent as the first American recipient of a Nobel Prize in any discipline.

Throughout his life, Roosevelt battled numerous health issues. His asthma continued to plague him, and he suffered injuries while boxing and during his adventurous expeditions. In 1912, while campaigning for a third term as President, Roosevelt was shot in the chest in an assassination attempt. Demonstrating extraordinary Stoicism, he delivered a 90-minute speech before seeking medical attention, famously stating, "It takes more than that to kill a Bull Moose."

Roosevelt's approach to life closely mirrored the principles of Stoicism, a philosophy that emphasizes virtue, endurance, and rationality in the face of hardship. Stoicism teaches the importance of self-control and fortitude as a means of overcoming destructive emotions. Roosevelt's life exemplified these ideals: his response to personal tragedies, his approach to physical ailments, and his unyielding commitment to his values and duties.

His resilience in the face of suffering, his commitment to living a life of virtue and service, and his ability to maintain composure and rationality in times of crisis are hallmarks of a stoic mindset. Roosevelt's legacy is not just in his political achievements or his contributions to American society but also in the Stoic manner in which he led his life, inspiring countless others to face their challenges with similar fortitude and resolve.

In conclusion, Theodore Roosevelt's journey was marked by numerous challenges, ranging from personal losses to physical afflictions. Yet, it was his stoic resolve that enabled him to transform these hardships into a source of strength. His life serves as a powerful illustration of how Stoic principles can guide one through the tumultuous waves of adversity, allowing for not just survival but triumph.

NINE

Stoic Secrets for Lasting Relationships

In the grand tapestry of life, relationships form the threads that weave together our shared human experience. They bring color to our existence, shape our identities, and influence our well-being. Yet, like any intricate tapestry, relationships can sometimes become tangled, strained, and fraught with complexities. How, then, does Stoicism, a philosophy rooted in ancient wisdom, guide us in navigating the intricacies of modern relationships? The answer lies in understanding the Stoic perspective on relationships and applying its principles to foster emotional balance, uphold virtue ethics, and cultivate compassion and empathy.

The Stoic Perspective on Relationships

Relationships, in their myriad forms, are an integral part of our lives. They offer companionship, support, and a sense of belonging, enriching our lives in countless ways. Yet, they can also be sources of conflict, misunderstanding, and emotional turmoil. The Stoic perspective on relationships provides a compass to navigate these challenges, guiding us towards healthier, more fulfilling interactions.

Stoic Indifference and Emotional Balance

When we think of indifference, we often associate it with apathy or disinterest, traits that seem contrary to the warmth and connection that relationships thrive on. However, the Stoic concept of indifference, or 'apatheia,' paints a different picture.

Stoic indifference is about maintaining emotional balance, regardless of external circumstances. It's about not letting our happiness or peace of mind overly depend on our relationships. This emotional balance doesn't mean we become cold or unfeeling. Instead, we learn to manage our emotions in a way that preserves our inner tranquility.

Imagine you're on a boat sailing on a choppy sea. The sea represents your relationships, full of ebbs and flows, highs and lows. If you allow the waves to toss your boat around, you'll likely end up feeling seasick. But if you learn to steer your boat skillfully, you can navigate the waves with balance and composure. That's what Stoic indifference brings to relationships - a sense of balance, a skillful steering of emotions that protects our inner peace.

Virtue Ethics in Relationships

In the realm of Stoicism, virtues form the bedrock of ethical living. They guide our actions, shape our character, and influence our interactions with others. When applied to relationships, virtue ethics provide a moral compass that steers us toward healthier, more harmonious interactions.

Consider the virtue of justice, which involves treating others with fairness, respect, and kindness. In a relationship, practicing justice could mean listening to your partner's perspective, respecting their boundaries, or making decisions considering their well-being.

The virtue of courage, which involves standing up for what's right, can guide us in addressing conflicts, setting boundaries, or supporting a loved one through a difficult time. The virtues of wisdom and temperance can help us make informed decisions, manage our emotions, and maintain balance in our relationships.

We cultivate healthier, more fulfilling interactions by upholding these virtues in our relationships. We build relationships that are not just emotionally satisfying but also morally enriching.

Stoic Compassion and Empathy

At first glance, Stoicism, with its emphasis on emotional control and indifference, might seem to advocate a lack of empathy or compassion. However, a closer look reveals that Stoicism deeply values these qualities and considers them integral to our relationships.

Stoic compassion is about understanding and acknowledging others' suffering without becoming emotionally overwhelmed. It's about offering support, not out of pity or a sense of duty, but out of a genuine understanding of our shared human experience.

Stoic empathy involves putting ourselves in another's shoes and understanding their perspective. It's about recognizing that, like us, others are navigating life's challenges, shaped by their unique circumstances and experiences.

Imagine you're watching a play. Each character has a role, script, and unique contribution to the story. But behind the characters, behind the masks, they're all actors, just like you - human beings navigating the grand stage of life. Stoic compassion and empathy are about seeing beyond the characters and recognizing the actors, the shared humanity, and the shared threads that connect us all of us.

We foster deeper connections, mutual understanding, and a sense of shared humanity by cultivating compassion and empathy in our relationships. We build relationships that are not just about give and take but about understanding and sharing to connect on a deeper, more meaningful level.

In the complex tapestry of relationships, Stoicism provides the threads of emotional balance, virtue ethics, and compassion, helping us weave healthier, more fulfilling interactions. It guides us in navigating the challenges of relationships, fostering understanding, harmony, and deep connections. As we continue our exploration of Stoicism, let's carry these threads with us, weaving them into our relationships and our lives, creating a tapestry that is as beautiful as it is resilient.

Stoic Strategies for Healthy Relationships

Stoicism, at its heart, is a practical philosophy offering actionable strategies that can be applied to various aspects of life, including relationships. These strategies, rooted in ancient wisdom, provide a roadmap for navigating the complex terrain of interpersonal interactions, fostering healthier, more fulfilling relationships. Let's explore three vital Stoic strategies for healthy relationships: practicing forgiveness, cultivating patience, and developing empathy.

Practicing Forgiveness

In the realm of relationships, hurt and misunderstanding are often inevitable. Yet, Stoicism teaches us that holding onto resentment and harboring grudges only leads to suffering and discord. Instead, it encourages the practice of forgiveness, a powerful act that can heal relationships and free us from the burden of resentment.

In the Stoic sense, forgiveness is not about condoning harmful behavior or ignoring injustice. It's about accepting the past, understanding human fallibility, and letting go of resentment for our peace of mind. It's about recognizing that while we can't change the past, we can control how we respond to it.

To practice forgiveness, start by reflecting on a situation where you felt wronged. Instead of dwelling on the hurt, try understanding the other person's perspective. Could their actions have been driven by ignorance, fear, or their own pain? This understanding can foster a sense of compassion, making forgiving easier.

Remember, forgiveness is a gift you give to yourself. It frees you from the prison of resentment, allowing you to live with a lighter heart and a clearer mind.

Cultivating Patience

Patience is another Stoic virtue that plays a vital role in relationships. Patience is often overlooked in a world that values speed and instant gratification. Yet, it's an essential ingredient for healthy relationships.

Patience involves accepting others as they are and giving them the space to grow at their own pace. It's about understanding that people like us are works in progress and that change takes time. It's about resisting the urge to rush, criticize, or control. Choose to be supportive, understanding, and patient instead.

To cultivate patience:

1. Try to catch yourself when you're becoming impatient.
2. Take a deep breath, and remember the Stoic principle of acceptance.
3. Remember, you can't control others or how fast they change, but you can manage your own responses.

By choosing patience, you select a path of understanding, acceptance, and love.

Developing Empathy

Empathy involves understanding and sharing other people's feelings and is a crucial aspect of Stoic compassion. It's about stepping into another's shoes, seeing the world through their eyes, and connecting with them on a deeper, emotional level.

Developing empathy involves active listening, open-mindedness, and a genuine interest in understanding others. It's about setting aside our judgments, assumptions, and preoccupations and being fully present with the other person. It's about recognizing our shared humanity, our everyday struggles, and our collective longing for understanding and connection.

To develop empathy, practice being fully present in your interactions. Listen attentively, ask open-ended questions, and show genuine interest in the other person's thoughts and feelings. Try to understand their point of view, even if it's different from yours. Remember, empathy is not about agreeing with others but about understanding them. Developing empathy builds deeper connections, fosters mutual understanding, and creates healthier, more fulfilling relationships.

In the intricate dance of relationships, Stoic strategies serve as our guide, leading us toward healthier, more harmonious interactions. They remind us that relationships, at their core, are about understanding, acceptance, and connection. They encourage us to practice forgiveness, cultivate patience, and develop empathy, transforming our relationships from a source of stress into a source of happiness and fulfillment. As we continue to explore the rich history of Stoicism, let these strategies serve as our compass, guiding our steps and enriching our dance in the grand ballroom of relationships.

Stoicism and Relationships: Case Study

Michelle and Barack Obama, whose marriage has been a subject of admiration and scrutiny, exemplify many Stoic virtues in their personal and public life. Their journey together, from humble beginnings to the highest echelons of political power, showcases a shared commitment to rationality, resilience, and mutual support - critical aspects of Stoic philosophy.

Michelle Obama, born on January 17, 1964, was raised in Chicago in a family that strongly emphasized the importance of education and diligent work. She excelled academically, attending Princeton University and Harvard Law School. Barack was born in Hawaii in 1961. He experienced a childhood of frequent relocations, moving between Hawaii and Indonesia. He also achieved academic success, which eventually led him to attend Harvard Law School. Their paths crossed at a law firm in Chicago, where Michelle was assigned as Barack's advisor. This meeting marked the beginning of a partnership that would eventually have a significant impact on American history.

Their early relationship was a test of balance and understanding - vital Stoic virtues. Barack's political aspirations required resilience and adaptability, both of which Michelle had to embrace. Stoicism teaches the importance of supporting one's partner through challenges, a principle they both exemplified as Barack entered the political arena, first as a state senator and then as a U.S. Senator.

Barack Obama's presidential campaign in 2008 was a period where both had to exhibit immense Stoic virtues. The campaign trail was grueling, and the scrutiny intense. They faced various challenges, including public criticism and intense media scrutiny. Throughout these trials, Michelle and Barack demonstrated the Stoic principle of focusing on what they could control: their actions, responses, and the integrity of their message.

During her time as First Lady, Michelle showed remarkable resilience and composure, qualities deeply valued in Stoicism. She championed causes like education, health, and military families, all while maintaining a balanced family life. The way she handled criticism and pressure, always responding with grace and thoughtfulness, is reflective of the Stoic idea of maintaining inner tranquility despite external turbulence.

Significant challenges, including economic crises, military conflicts, and intense political polarization, marked Barack Obama's Presidency. His calm demeanor, especially in times of crisis, echoed the Stoic ideal of maintaining composure and rationality in the face of adversity. He often spoke about the importance of empathy, understanding, and looking at the bigger picture - principles that resonate with Stoic ethics.

Their relationship, particularly during the Presidency, also reflected Stoic virtues. They maintained a solid and supportive partnership, often speaking about the importance of communication, understanding each other's perspectives, and supporting each other's individual growth. This mutual respect and understanding are crucial in Stoic relationships, where the focus is on rational companionship and emotional resilience.

Post-presidency, both Michelle and Barack have continued to exhibit Stoic virtues. Michelle's memoir, "Becoming," is a testament to her journey of self-discovery, growth, and resilience. Barack's post-presidential endeavors, focusing on issues like democracy, leadership, and social change, reflect a continued commitment to Stoic ideals of wisdom, justice, and contributing to the greater good.

In conclusion, individually and as a couple, Michelle and Barack Obama's life journey is marked by the application of Stoic virtues. Their ability to navigate the complexities of their careers, the challenges of the Presidency, and their continued work in public life with resilience, rationality, and a commitment to ethical principles showcases how Stoic philosophy can be relevant and impactful in modern relationships and public life. Their story is not just one of political and personal achievement but also an illustration of how enduring principles of Stoicism can guide and strengthen a partnership through the diverse challenges of life.

Reflecting on Relationships: Journaling Exercises

Dealing with the complexities of relationships can often feel like sailing in uncharted waters. Yet, with its timeless wisdom and practical strategies, Stoicism provides us with a reliable compass. Let's engage with some reflective journaling exercises to delve deeper into this compass and integrate its guidance into our relationships.

Journaling on Indifference in Relationships

Making decisions when you're angry is often a decision you will regret. The first exercise focuses on the concept of Stoic indifference, a principle that encourages us to maintain emotional balance in our relationships. To begin, think of a situation in your personal life where you felt emotionally unbalanced. It could be a disagreement with a friend, a family conflict, or a romantic relationship issue.

Describe the situation in your journal, focusing on the emotions it stirred in you. Now, consider the Stoic principle of indifference. Reflect on how you would have responded to this situation if you maintained emotional balance.

Write about this balanced response in your journal. How would it have influenced your actions, your emotions, and the outcome of the situation? Reflecting on this can provide valuable insights into maintaining emotional balance in your relationships, fostering healthier, more harmonious interactions.

Writing About Virtues in Relationships

The second exercise explores the role of virtues in our relationships. Begin by identifying a virtue you wish to cultivate in your relationships. It could be patience, kindness, honesty, or any other virtue you value.

Reflect on why this virtue is essential to you and how it can enhance your relationships. Write about a recent interaction where you could have demonstrated this virtue. How would it have influenced the interaction? How would it have affected the other person's feelings and your relationship with them?

By writing about virtues in this way, we gain a better understanding of their importance and create a roadmap for practicing them in our relationships. This practice can foster healthier, more fulfilling interactions and build relationships that are not just emotionally satisfying but also morally enriching.

Reflecting on Compassion and Empathy

The final exercise invites you to reflect on the role of compassion and empathy in your relationships. Compassion involves understanding and acknowledging others' suffering, while empathy involves sharing their feelings and understanding their perspective.

Think about a situation where someone you care about was going through a difficult time. Write about this situation in your journal, and reflect on how you responded. Did you demonstrate compassion and empathy? How did it affect the other person and your relationship with them?

By reflecting on compassion and empathy, we can understand their significance in our relationships and strive to embody them in our interactions. These qualities can deepen our connections, foster mutual understanding, and create healthier, more fulfilling relationships with the people around us.

The act of journaling, while simple, can be immensely powerful. It provides a space for reflection, introspection, and personal growth. It allows us to engage with Stoic principles on a deeper level and integrate them into our relationships. So, pick up your pen and start journaling. Explore emotional balance, delve into virtues, and reflect on compassion and empathy. Through your words, you're not only deepening your understanding of Stoicism but also enriching your relationships, one reflection at a time.

As we leave this exploration of Stoicism and relationships, let's carry forward the insights we've gained, the reflections we've made, and the growth we've experienced. As we move forward, let's strive to weave the threads of Stoicism into the tapestry of our relationships, creating a pattern that's as beautiful as it is resilient. Onward, then, to the next chapter of our exploration, where we will delve into the impact of digital distractions on our lives and how Stoicism can help us navigate this modern-day challenge.

TEN

Living Mindfully in The Digital Age

In our ever-connected world, where smartphones buzz with notifications, social media feeds never cease to update, and digital distractions are just a click away, finding tranquility can feel like a quest for a hidden treasure. Yet, with its timeless wisdom, Stoicism offers us a map to this treasure. It provides principles and practices that equip us to navigate the digital age with equanimity, mindfulness, and a deep sense of fulfillment.

Stoicism in the Digital Age

Dichotomy of Control and Digital Consumption

The principle of the dichotomy of control is one of the cornerstones of Stoicism. It teaches us to distinguish between what is within our control and what is not and to focus our energy and attention on the former.

In the context of digital consumption, this principle takes on a new significance. Consider your own digital habits. The buzz of a smartphone, the glow of a screen, and the allure of social media are external factors outside your control. However, how you respond to these distractions, how much time you spend on digital platforms, and how you let these digital interactions affect your mood and focus are within your control.

Embracing the dichotomy of control in digital consumption empowers you to manage your digital habits effectively. Instead of being swept away by the tide of digital distractions, you can choose to surf the waves, deciding when to engage and when to step back. This shift in perspective can reduce stress, enhance productivity, and foster a sense of digital well-being.

Virtue Ethics in Digital Communication

In the virtual world, where communication happens at the click of a button, and conversations span across continents, upholding virtue ethics becomes both a challenge and a necessity. In the Stoic sense, virtue ethics involves living following virtues like wisdom, courage, justice, and temperance.

Applying virtue ethics to digital communication means bringing these virtues into our online interactions. Wisdom can guide us to responsibly share and consume digital content, discerning reliable information from misinformation. Courage can inspire us to voice our opinions respectfully, stand against online harassment, and uphold fundamental integrity. Justice can lead us to treat all individuals fairly and kindly in the digital space, recognizing the dignity and worth behind each username and profile picture. Temperance can help us maintain a balanced approach to digital consumption, preventing us from falling into the trap of digital addiction.

By embodying these virtues in digital communication, we can foster healthier, more meaningful online interactions. We can use digital platforms as tools for connection, learning, and growth rather than letting them use us.

Stoic Mindfulness in the Digital World

Mindfulness is the art of being fully present and engaged in the current moment. It aligns closely with Stoic philosophy. In the digital age, where screens often fragment our attention and digital notifications constantly pull us away from the present, Stoic mindfulness offers a counterbalance.

Practicing Stoic mindfulness in the digital world involves being conscious of our digital habits, observing them without judgment, and making mindful choices. It might mean turning off unnecessary notifications, setting aside gadget-free times, or mindfully focusing on one digital task at a time instead of succumbing to digital multitasking.

This mindfulness practice can enable us to use digital tools without becoming enslaved by them. It can help us navigate the digital world with a clear mind, focused attention, and a sense of purpose, transforming our digital experience from a source of distraction to a platform for growth.

In the digital age, where our attention is the new currency, Stoicism offers invaluable wealth. It equips us with the mindset and tools to manage digital distractions, communicate virtuously, and cultivate mindfulness. It transforms our digital experience from a chaotic cacophony into a symphony of growth, connection, and purpose. With Stoicism as our guide, we can sail the digital seas with skill and confidence, discovering treasures of wisdom, virtue, and fulfillment along the way.

Strategies for Digital Detox

Stoic philosophy emphasizes mindfulness, the practice of being fully present and engaged in the current moment. This mindfulness can offer a refreshing perspective on our social media use.

Mindful social media use involves being fully aware of our actions, reactions, and emotions while using social media. It's about using social media intentionally, not habitually. It's noticing how much time we spend scrolling through feeds, how we feel during and after our social media use, and how our social media habits affect our overall well-being.

The goal is to use social media with a clear intention and an acute awareness of its impact on us. It is good to question our digital habits, strive to make conscious choices, and use social media to enhance, not diminish our well-being.

Scheduled Digital Detox

In the realm of Stoicism, moderation is an essential virtue. It teaches us the value of balance and the wisdom in avoiding extremes. This principle of moderation can be applied to our digital habits through the practice of a Scheduled Digital Detox.

A Scheduled Digital Detox is essentially setting aside specific time slots in your daily routine where you intentionally disconnect from digital devices. It could be the first hour after you wake up, the last hour before you go to bed, or any other time that suits your schedule. The goal is to give your mind a much-needed break from the constant waves of digital information and distractions.

Try to schedule your digital detox in the morning when you wake up. This way, you will not let the noise from social media dictate what mood you start your day in. This practice is not about completely shunning digital technology. Instead, it's about using it to serve us, not enslave us. It's about reclaiming our time, attention, and peace of mind from the clutches of constant digital stimuli.

Stoic Reflections on Digital Consumption

Reflecting on our digital consumption is akin to holding up a mirror to our digital habits. This reflection can provide valuable insights into our digital behaviors, attitudes, and dependencies.

Stoic Reflections on Digital Consumption involve examining our digital habits honestly and openly. It's about acknowledging the impact of these habits on our mental health, productivity, and relationships. It's about recognizing our digital dependencies and exploring ways to reduce them.

This reflection is not an exercise in self-criticism or guilt. Instead, it's an opportunity for self-awareness, self-understanding, and self-improvement. It's a chance to realign our digital habits with our values, needs, and well-being. Keep track of your daily use of social media apps. If you know how long you spend mindlessly scrolling, you can aim to lower that time.

We can cultivate a healthier relationship with digital technology by reflecting on our digital consumption. We can use it as a tool to connect, learn, and grow rather than letting it control us. We can navigate the digital world with clarity, purpose, and a deep sense of fulfillment.

In the labyrinth of the digital age, Stoicism serves as our compass, guiding us toward healthier digital habits, mindful interactions, and a balanced digital lifestyle. It equips us with the mindset and strategies to navigate the digital landscape with a deep sense of purpose. With Stoicism as our guide, we can traverse the digital realm confidently and efficiently, discovering treasures of connection, growth, and well-being amidst the digital chaos.

What the Ancient Stoics Can Teach Us About the Digital Age

Marcus Aurelius and Information Overload

The reign of Marcus Aurelius is identified by his thoughtful and mindful approach to leadership. Much like we are today, he was inundated with a sea of information. As an emperor, he was expected to make decisions on various issues, each demanding his attention and understanding.

Navigating through this information overload, Marcus Aurelius found solace in the Stoic principles. He focused on what was within his control—his decisions, his responses, and his actions. He practiced Stoic mindfulness, concentrating on the task at hand and not allowing his mind to be scattered by the constant influx of information.

Marcus Aurelius' strategy for dealing with information overload is a beacon for us in today's digital age. His practice of mindfulness and focus on his sphere of control reflect the Stoic approach to managing digital distractions. In a world where we are constantly bombarded with notifications, messages, and updates, we can take a leaf out of Marcus Aurelius' book and practice mindfulness, focusing our attention on what truly matters and what is within our control.

Seneca and Leisure Time

Seneca, the Stoic statesman and philosopher, lived in a time when leisure was considered an opportunity for personal growth and learning. He was a staunch advocate of using leisure time wisely to engage in contemplation, self-improvement, and the study of philosophy.

In today's digital age, digital distractions often consume our leisure time. We scroll through social media feeds, binge-watch TV series, or get lost in the rabbit hole of online content. While these activities can provide temporary amusement, they often do not contribute to our long-term growth or well-being.

Seneca's approach to leisure time offers a valuable lesson for us. Instead of mindlessly consuming digital content, we can choose to use our leisure time for activities that enrich our lives and align with our values. This could include reading a book, practicing a hobby, spending time in nature, or learning a new skill. By doing so, we enhance our well-being and lead a more fulfilling and meaningful life, following the Stoic path.

Epictetus and Discourses in the Digital Age

Epictetus, the former slave turned Stoic philosopher, believed in the power of discourse and learning. His teachings, compiled in the form of dialogues and discussions, highlight the importance of open communication, active listening, and critical thinking.

In the digital age, we often engage in passive consumption of information. We read posts, listen to podcasts, and watch videos but rarely take the time to reflect on what we consume, question its validity, or engage in meaningful discussions.

The 'Discourses' of Epictetus remind us of the value of active engagement with digital content. Instead of passively consuming information, we can engage in digital discourses, question what we read or hear, and share our perspectives. This enhances our understanding and fosters a culture of open dialogue and critical thinking in the digital sphere.

Epictetus' approach to learning and discourse offers a refreshingly active and engaged approach to digital consumption. It encourages us to be mindful of what we consume, question, reflect, and engage. It inspires us to be active participants in the digital world, not just passive consumers.

In the vast digital landscape, Stoicism offers us a roadmap to navigate with wisdom, mindfulness, and purpose. The case studies of Marcus Aurelius, Seneca, and Epictetus illuminate this roadmap, offering valuable lessons on managing information overload, using leisure time wisely, and actively engaging with digital content. As we navigate the digital world, these Stoic lighthouses guide us toward a path of mindful digital consumption, meaningful digital interactions, and a fulfilling digital life.

Digital Detox Prompts: Journaling Exercises

The art of writing has long been a tool for self-discovery, introspection, and personal growth. In the realm of Stoic philosophy, writing can serve as a practical avenue to explore, apply, and internalize Stoic principles. As we navigate the digital landscape, let's turn to writing as our ally, guide, and tool for comprehension and transformation. Here are some Stoic writing exercises to foster healthier digital habits, enhance our digital interactions, and cultivate a mindful approach to our digital lives.

Reflecting on Your Digital Realm: Control and Consumption

Begin by pondering your digital habits. How much time do you devote to the digital world each day? How does this digital immersion affect your mood, focus, and overall well-being? Write about your digital life in your journal, painting a vivid picture of your digital habits and their impact on your life.

Next, delve into the Stoic principle of the dichotomy of control. Reflect on which aspects of your digital life are within your control (your digital consumption, your reactions to digital content, your digital contributions) and which are not (the behavior of others online, the digital content available, the digital norms of society). Write about these reflections in your journal, distinguishing between what you can control and what you can't in your digital life.

By journaling about control and digital consumption, we cultivate a Stoic approach to our digital lives. We focus our energy and attention on the things that truly matter and what is within our control, fostering healthier digital habits and a more fulfilling digital experience.

Virtuous Communication in the Digital World

Consider the digital communications in which you engage. How do you interact with others in the digital realm? How do you express your thoughts, opinions, and emotions? Are your digital communications a reflection of your values and principles? Write about these aspects in your journal, critically examining your digital communications.

Now, ponder the role of virtues in digital communication. Reflect on how you can embody the virtues of wisdom, courage, justice, and temperance in your digital interactions. How can wisdom guide your digital communications? How can courage inspire you to voice your thoughts respectfully? How can justice lead you to treat all individuals fairly in the digital space? How can temperance help you maintain a balanced approach to digital communication? Write about these reflections in your journal, exploring how virtue ethics can enhance your digital communications.

By journaling about virtues in digital communication, we align our online interactions with our values. We foster healthier digital communications, enhancing our digital relationships and building a more positive digital environment.

The Practice of Mindfulness in the Digital Universe

Reflect on your level of mindfulness when engaging with the digital world. Are you fully present when you're online, or is your mind elsewhere while you scroll for hours? Do you consume digital content intentionally or out of habit? What type of content do you consume? And why? Write about your experience with mindfulness in the digital world, exploring your level of presence and intentionality.

Now, consider how you can enhance your mindfulness in your digital life. Reflect on strategies such as setting intentional digital goals, practicing mindful browsing, or taking mindful breaks from digital devices. How can these strategies enhance your digital mindfulness? Write about these reflections in your journal, exploring ways to cultivate mindfulness in your digital life.

Journaling about digital mindfulness brings a sense of presence and intentionality to our digital lives. We transform our digital experience from a source of distraction into a platform for growth.

In the digital landscape where distractions abound, these writing exercises serve as lighthouses, guiding us towards healthier digital habits, meaningful digital interactions, and mindful digital living. As we put pen to paper, we acquire a deeper understanding of Stoicism and translate this understanding into our digital lives. We transform our digital experience from a source of stress into a source of growth, connection, and fulfillment. The exercises are simple: pick up your pen and start journaling. Explore control, delve into virtues, and ponder mindfulness. Through your words, you're not only deepening your understanding of Stoicism but also enriching your digital life, one reflection at a time.

With these reflections, we can navigate the often turbulent seas of digital life, steering our ship with the compass of Stoicism.

We have discovered treasures of wisdom, virtue, and mindfulness amidst the digital chaos. As we continue to sail, let's carry these treasures with us, integrating them into our everyday lives, enriching not just our digital experience but our human experience. Let's continue on this exploration, charting our course towards the next beacon of Stoic wisdom - the realm of personal setbacks.

ELEVEN

Turn Your Setbacks Into Opportunities

Life, in all its unpredictability, often resembles a game of chess. We strategize and make our moves with care, yet, at times, we find ourselves in a checkmate situation. Setbacks, failures, and disappointments corner us, threatening our peace and serenity. But rather than conceding defeat, we can turn to Stoicism, a philosophy that equips us with the mindset to turn setbacks into setups for comebacks.

With Stoicism as our ally, we can face life's challenges not with dread but with courage and resilience. When setbacks arrive, as they inevitably do, we don't lose heart. Instead, we respond with wisdom guided by the principles of Stoicism. Let's explore the Stoic approach to setbacks, delving into the dichotomy of control, virtue ethics, and resilience.

The Stoic Approach to Failure and Setbacks

The Dichotomy of Control in Facing Setbacks

When a setback strikes, feeling a sense of loss and disappointment is natural. However, the Stoic principle of the dichotomy of control invites us to view setbacks from a different perspective. This principle distinguishes between what's within our control - our actions, attitudes, and responses - and what's not - the setbacks themselves and their immediate outcomes.

Imagine you've been diligently working on a project at work, pouring your efforts into it, only to have it canceled due to budget cuts. The cancellation of the project, an external event, is beyond your control. But your response to this setback - whether you choose to wallow in disappointment or take it in stride, learn from the experience, and move on to the next challenge - is within your control.

Focusing on what's within our control allows us to navigate setbacks with a greater sense of calm and resilience. We learn to accept the setbacks, adapt to new circumstances, and continue moving forward, guided by our values and commitment to personal growth.

Virtue Ethics in Overcoming Failure

Stoicism emphasizes the importance of living in sync with virtue, regardless of external circumstances. In the face of setbacks, this commitment to virtue becomes our guiding light, illuminating the path forward.

Consider the virtue of courage. It urges us to face our setbacks head-on, to confront our fears and uncertainties, and to persist in our efforts despite the difficulties. It's like a climber scaling a steep mountain. Despite the challenges, the climber continues, driven by courage and a determination to reach the summit.

Another critical virtue is wisdom, which involves making well-informed decisions and responding to situations with discernment. When faced with a setback, wisdom guides us to learn from the experience, to understand what went wrong and how we can improve, and to make better decisions moving forward.

By cultivating these virtues, we equip ourselves to handle setbacks more effectively. We learn to see failure not as a dead-end but as a detour, a stepping stone on our path to growth and self-improvement.

Stoic Resilience in Life's Challenges

Resilience, in the Stoic sense, is not about avoiding setbacks or returning to our original state. It's about bouncing forward, growing stronger and wiser from our experiences. It's about transforming setbacks into opportunities for learning and growth.

Imagine a tree during a storm. The winds are strong, and the tree bends under their force. But when the storm passes, the tree doesn't just bounce back to its original position. It grows new roots to stabilize itself, it repairs its broken branches, and it springs forth new leaves. That's resilience in the Stoic sense - a process of continual growth and adaptation fueled by the challenges we encounter.

When we face setbacks, Stoicism encourages us to embrace this resilience. Instead of resisting the setback, we learn from it. Instead of dwelling on the loss, we focus on the lessons. And instead of yearning for our old state, we strive to grow into a stronger, wiser version of ourselves.

In the game of life, setbacks may corner us, but Stoicism equips us to make our next move with composure, wisdom, and resilience. It reminds us that the true game is not about avoiding setbacks but about how we respond to them. It's about playing our best game, regardless of the challenges we face, and emerging stronger, wiser, and more resilient with each move.

Turning Setbacks Into Opportunities: Case Study One

Nelson Mandela was an inspiring figure in the fight against apartheid in South Africa. He exemplifies the stoic virtues of resilience, perseverance, and the ability to turn setbacks into opportunities. His journey from a prison inmate to a world-renowned statesman is a testament to his unyielding spirit and commitment to his cause.

Mandela, born in 1918 in South Africa's Eastern Cape, was greatly influenced by his ancestors' heroic tales during resistance wars. He attended Fort Hare University and the University of Witwatersrand, where he studied law. Mandela's early experiences with racial discrimination and injustice ignited his lifelong dedication to fighting apartheid, a framework of institutionalized racial segregation and discrimination in South Africa.

Mandela officially became a part of the African National Congress in 1944. It is a political party committed to ending apartheid. He quickly rose through its ranks, becoming a leader of its youth wing. Non-violent protests marked his early activism. However, as the South African government's repression intensified, Mandela and other ANC leaders began to believe that armed struggle was the only path to change. It led to the formation of Umkhonto we Sizwe (Spear of the Nation), the armed wing of the ANC.

In 1962, Mandela faced arrest and a life sentence for leading the fight against apartheid. He endured 27 years of imprisonment, predominantly on Robben Island, under severe conditions. His imprisonment involved living in a small cell without basic amenities, performing strenuous labor in a lime quarry, and facing cruel treatment from guards. Through all these challenges, Mandela's determination never wavered.

Mandela's Stoicism was evident in his conduct during his imprisonment. He consistently demonstrated self-discipline, emotional control, and unwavering commitment to his principles. He used his time in prison to deepen his understanding of the enemy, the Afrikaners, learning their language and studying their culture. Mandela also engaged in clandestine negotiations with the apartheid regime, showing a pragmatic approach to finding a peaceful solution to the country's racial strife.

The stoic idea of focusing on what can be controlled and accepting what cannot be changed was central to Mandela's approach. He worked on improving himself, pursuing a Bachelor of Law degree by correspondence, and was a mentor to younger prisoners, earning the nickname 'Madiba' (a term of respect). Even under the most oppressive circumstances, he maintained his dignity and leadership role, embodying the stoic virtues of endurance and moral integrity.

Mandela's release in 1990 marked the beginning of a new era in South Africa's history. He led the ANC in negotiations with President F.W. de Klerk to dismantle apartheid. This resulted in the 1994 multi-racial general elections, in which Mandela was elected South Africa's first Black president.

As president, Mandela focused on reconciliation, not retribution, exemplifying another stoic virtue: the ability to forgive and seek harmony. He worked tirelessly to unite a country divided by decades of racial hatred, establishing the Truth and Reconciliation Commission to help heal the nation. Mandela's presidency was identified by his efforts to dismantle the legacy of apartheid by tackling institutionalized racism, poverty, and inequality.

Stoicism played a vital role in Mandela's journey. His ability to endure suffering without succumbing to hatred or bitterness, his focus on rational and pragmatic solutions to complex problems, and his commitment to moral principles in the face of overwhelming challenges were all deeply stoic. Mandela's life illustrates how setbacks can be transformed into opportunities to grow, lead, and effect significant change.

In conclusion, Nelson Mandela's story is one of remarkable resilience and transformation. His journey from a political prisoner to a celebrated nation leader is a narrative of how personal suffering can be transcended for the greater good. Mandela's embodiment of stoic virtues—endurance, self-discipline, rationality, and commitment to justice—was instrumental in his survival and profound impact on the world. His legacy continues to be a lighthouse for people who seek to overcome adversity with dignity, strength, and an unwavering commitment to higher principles.

Turning Setbacks Into Opportunities: Case Study Two

Jack Ma, the charismatic Chinese entrepreneur and founder of Alibaba, one of the world's largest e-commerce platforms, is a quintessential example of turning setbacks into opportunities, embodying many principles of Stoicism in his journey.

Born Ma Yun in 1964, in Hangzhou, Zhejiang province, China, Jack Ma's early life was marked by adversity and challenges. He grew up in a period of economic turmoil and political upheaval during the Cultural Revolution in China. Despite his humble beginnings and facing academic setbacks - he failed his college entrance exam twice - Ma persevered, eventually enrolling at Hangzhou Teacher's Institute and graduating with a Bachelor's degree in English.

Ma's foray into the business world was fraught with failures and rejections, a theme that would continue throughout his early career. Famously, he applied for 30 jobs and was rejected by all, including a job at KFC. In 1995, while on a trip to the US, Ma was introduced to the internet, a moment that changed his life. Fascinated by this new technology, he returned to China with a vision to create an internet company for Chinese users.

He started his first venture, China Yellowpages, which is considered to be China's first internet-based company, but it struggled to make a profit. Undeterred, Ma continued to explore the possibilities of the internet. In 1999, he assembled 17 of his friends in his home and persuaded them to invest in his concept for an online marketplace, which he named "Alibaba." The idea was to create a platform allowing Chinese manufacturers to connect with international buyers.

Alibaba's early days were challenging. The company faced stiff competition, a lack of funding, and skepticism about the viability of e-commerce in China. Despite these obstacles, Ma's unwavering belief in his vision and his ability to inspire his team kept the company afloat. He famously advocated for a customer-first approach, insisting that trust and user experience were paramount for the platform's success.

Jack Ma's Stoicism is evident in his resilience and his philosophical approach to failure and success. He often speaks about the importance of learning from mistakes and seeing challenges as opportunities to improve and adapt. This mindset is deeply stoic, reflecting the philosophy's emphasis on personal growth through adversity.

Under Ma's leadership, Alibaba saw remarkable growth. In 2003, the company launched Taobao, a site for small businesses and individual entrepreneurs to sell their goods, which quickly dominated the Chinese online retail market. This was followed by the creation of Alipay, a secure payment system that addressed the lack of trust in online transactions, a crucial step in cultivating the e-commerce ecosystem in China.

In 2014, Alibaba made history with the largest initial public offering (IPO) ever, raising $25 billion on the New York Stock Exchange. This success was not just a testament to the company's financial prowess but also to Ma's vision and ability to persist despite skepticism and setbacks.

Throughout his career, Jack Ma has demonstrated a stoic attitude in dealing with both success and failure. He emphasizes the importance of emotional balance, the value of learning from hardships, and the necessity of maintaining humility and focus in the face of success. His approach to leadership and life reflects the stoic belief in self-control, rational decision-making, and the pursuit of a greater good.

In later years, Ma transitioned from his role at Alibaba to focus on philanthropy, education, and environmental causes, reflecting the stoic ideal of using one's influence to improve society.

In conclusion, Jack Ma's life story is an example of the power of resilience, vision, and the stoic philosophy of turning setbacks into opportunities. From his humble beginnings and numerous rejections to leading one of the most successful e-commerce giants in the world, Ma's journey exemplifies how enduring adversity, maintaining a balanced perspective on success and failure, and focusing on continuous personal and professional growth can lead to extraordinary achievements. His legacy is a thriving business empire and an inspiring narrative about the transformative power of a stoic mindset in the face of seemingly insurmountable challenges.

Reflective Prompts for Overcoming Setbacks: Journaling Exercises

Journaling on Control in Facing Setbacks

As we navigate the labyrinth of life, setbacks often appear like towering walls, blocking our path and casting long shadows of doubt and despair. Yet, the Stoic principle of the dichotomy of control provides us with a ladder to climb over these walls.

Get hold of your journal, and think about a recent setback you encountered. It could be a professional challenge, a personal disappointment, or a failed endeavor. Describe the situation in your journal, detailing the emotions, thoughts, and reactions it stirred within you.

Next, apply the dichotomy of control to this setback. Identify the elements within your control - your actions, reactions, and attitude toward the setback. Then, pinpoint the elements that were beyond your control - the setback itself, the circumstances leading to it, the immediate outcomes.

Reflect on how you responded to these uncontrollable elements. Did you resist them, causing yourself unnecessary stress and disappointment? Or did you accept them, focusing instead on what was within your control? Write about your reflections in your journal, exploring how you can better apply the dichotomy of control in future setbacks.

Writing About Virtues in Overcoming Failure

In the theater of life, failures often play the antagonist, casting us into the depths of despair and self-doubt. However, Stoicism teaches us to view failures not as villains but as challenging scripts, pushing us to deliver our best performance. It directs us towards the virtues of courage and wisdom, helping us navigate failure with bravery and insight.

Open your journal, and think about a recent failure you experienced. Write about this failure, describing how it made you feel, how it affected your self-esteem, and how it influenced your subsequent actions.

Now, bring the virtues of courage and wisdom into the picture. Reflect on how courage could have helped you face the failure head-on without fear or shame. Consider how wisdom could have guided you to learn from failure, understand its causes, and make better future decisions.

Write about these reflections in your journal. Consider how embodying these virtues can change your perspective on failure, transforming it from a source of fear into a source of growth and self-improvement.

Reflecting on Resilience in Life's Challenges

Life, with its twists and turns, often feels like a rocky road filled with potholes of challenges and setbacks. Yet, the Stoic concept of resilience equips us with a robust vehicle to traverse this road, turning every pothole into a milestone on our journey of personal growth.

Grab your journal, and reflect on a recent challenge you faced. It could be a conflict at work, a health issue, or a personal crisis. Write about this challenge, detailing your initial reactions, coping strategies, and the impact on your life.

Next, reflect on your resilience in the face of this challenge. Did you bounce back from the setback? Did you grow from the experience? Did you learn new lessons and acquire new skills? Did the challenge spur you to make positive changes in your life?

Write about your reflections in your journal. Reflect on how you can enhance your resilience, using every challenge as an opportunity to grow stronger, wiser, and more resilient.

As we conclude this chapter, let us remember that setbacks, failures, and challenges are not dead-ends on our path but signposts guiding us toward personal growth. They are opportunities to apply the principles of Stoicism, to practice the dichotomy of control, to uphold virtue ethics, and to cultivate resilience. They are the sparks that ignite our growth, the grit that polishes our strength, and the winds that lift us higher. As we continue our exploration of Stoicism, let's carry these insights with us, using them as our compass to navigate life's challenges and embark on a fulfilling journey of personal growth.

Epilogue

Revisiting the Journey: The Path Walked and the Lessons Learned

As we stand on the threshold of the end of this journey, let's pause and look back at the path we have traversed. Together, we have ventured into the realm of Stoicism, a philosophy that has stood the test of time, weathering the storms of change and transition.

We began our exploration by understanding the origins and principles of Stoicism, unveiling the wisdom of the Stoic masters such as Marcus Aurelius, Epictetus, and Seneca. We then embarked on a quest to apply these principles to our modern lives, delving into topics such as emotional regulation, resilience, confidence, relationships, and the digital world.

Together, we confronted setbacks, navigated emotional landscapes, and discovered the power of virtues like wisdom, courage, justice, and temperance. We explored how Stoicism can guide us to live in harmony with the natural world, to focus on what we can control, and to cultivate a deep sense of fulfillment.

Stoicism in Your Hands: A Tool for Life

As we reach the end of our journey, remember that the wisdom of Stoicism is now a tool in your hands, a compass to guide you through life's challenges and triumphs. And like any tool, it becomes more effective with practice.

Lean on Stoicism when you face setbacks, drawing upon its teachings to transform these obstacles into opportunities for growth. Use it as a guide to cultivate emotional balance, navigate your relationships with grace, and build resilience. Let it be your beacon in the digital world, guiding you to use technology mindfully and productively.

The Path Ahead: Continuing Your Stoic Journey

As we step off the pages of this book, remember that your Stoic journey is far from over. Stoicism is more than a philosophy to be studied; it is a way of life to be lived. Like any journey, it is a continuous process of learning, reflection, and growth.

As you continue to explore Stoicism in your everyday life, apply its principles to new challenges. Reflect on its teachings. Share your insights with others. Let your Stoic journey shape, guide, and inspire you to become the best version of yourself.

Final Thoughts: Embrace Stoicism, Embrace Life

Stoicism, in its quiet, unassuming way, invites us to embrace life in all its complexity. It encourages us to view the world with a sense of curiosity, to face challenges with courage, to cultivate virtues, and to live in harmony with nature.

So, as we part ways, I leave you with this thought: Embrace Stoicism, and you embrace life itself. You embrace the challenges and the triumphs, the highs and the lows, the joys and the sorrows. Furthermore, in doing so, you open yourself to a life of wisdom, virtue, and fulfillment.

Thank you for joining me on this journey. May your path be illuminated by the wisdom of Stoicism, and may your life be filled with courage, wisdom, justice, and temperance. As you continue your journey, remember the words of Marcus Aurelius, "The happiness of your life depends upon the quality of your thoughts." May your thoughts be guided by virtue, enlightened by wisdom, and rooted in the present moment.

Thus, I bid you farewell with a heart full of gratitude and a spirit brimming with Stoic wisdom. Carry forth the torch of Stoicism, let it light your path, and shine its light for others to see. Here is to your journey, to your growth, and to the wisdom that lies within you!

Resources

Applying Stoicism: The Stoic Career by Travis Hume. (2017, February 4). Modern Stoicism. https://modernstoicism.com/applying-stoicism-the-stoic-career-by-travis-hume/

Attainataraxia. (2016, March 7). Comparing and contrasting the stoicism of Seneca, Epictetus, and Marcus Aurelius. THE EDUCATION OF A MILLENNIAL. https://educationofamillennial.wordpress.com/2016/03/07/comparing-and-contrasting-the-stoicism-of-seneca-epictetus-and-marcus-aurelius/

Billy. (2020, February 27). 12 Lessons on Leadership from the Last Great Emperor. Daily Stoic. https://dailystoic.com/12-lessons-on-leadership-from-the-last-great-emperor/

Cato the Younger: Rome's last Republican and his deadly fight against Julius Caesar's tyranny. (n.d.). History Skills. https://www.historyskills.com/classroom/ancient-history/cato-the-younger/

Daily Stoic. (2023, April 18). Stoic quotes: The best quotes from the Stoics. https://dailystoic.com/stoic-quotes/

Darabán, I. (2023, September 12). The Stoics were right – emotional control is good for the soul. Psyche. https://psyche.co/ideas/the-stoics-were-right-emotional-control-is-good-for-the-soul

Epictetus (Stanford Encyclopedia of Philosophy). (2021, June 15). https://plato.stanford.edu/entries/epictetus/

Eternalised. (2021, May 3). *How to practice stoicism in daily life | Modern Stoic. Eternalised.* https://eternalisedofficial.com/2020/08/29/how-to-practice-stoicism-in-daily-life/

Gnaulati, E., Ph.D. (2023, July 24). *The clinical uses of stoic acceptance - Mad in America. Made in America.* https://www.madinamerica.com/2023/07/stoic-acceptance/

Happy Families: A Stoic Guide to Family Relationships by Brittany Polat. (2017, November 4). Modern Stoicism. https://modernstoicism.com/happy-families-a-stoic-guide-to-family-relationships-by-brittany-polat/

Holiday, R. (2017a, August 2). *Control and choice. Daily Stoic.* https://dailystoic.com/control-and-choice/

Holiday, R. (2017b, August 8). *3 Practical and effective stoic exercises from Marcus Aurelius, Seneca, and Epictetus. Daily Stoic.* https://dailystoic.com/practical-stoic-exercises/

Holiday, R. (2017c, November 25). *A stoic response to failure. Daily Stoic.* https://dailystoic.com/stoic-response-failure/

Holiday, R. (2022a, March 7). *10 Insanely useful stoic exercises. Daily Stoic.* https://dailystoic.com/10-insanely-useful-stoic-exercises/

Holiday, R. (2022b, August 31). *12 Extraordinary Stoic Moments - Ryan Holiday - Medium. Medium.* https://ryanholiday.medium.com/12-extraordinary-stoic-moments-95d263b48530

How CBT can help with Internet Addiction. (n.d.). https://rehabsuk.com/addictions/behavioural/cbt-for-internet-addiction/

How Stoicism Could Help You Build Resilience. (n.d.). Psychology Today. https://www.psychologytoday.com/us/blog/the-psychology-stoicism/202208/how-stoicism-could-help-you-build-resilience

Journaling as a recovery and resilience building tool - CoBb Collaborative. (n.d.). Cobb Collaborative. https://www.cobbcollaborative.org/journaling-as-a-recovery-and-resilience-building-tool

Konstan, D. (2015). Senecan emotions. In Cambridge University Press eBooks (pp. 174–184). https://doi.org/10.1017/cco9781139542746.016

Lake, T. (2023, November 15). An in-depth understanding on the four virtues of stoicism. TheCollector. https://www.thecollector.com/four-cardinal-virtues-stoicism/#:~:text=Seneca's%20courage%20to%20face%20his,to%20what%20Socrates%20had%20done.

MacRae, B. (2023, June 6). How to practice the virtue of temperance in stoicism. The Mindful Stoic. https://mindfulstoic.net/applying-temperance/

Man's search for meaning. (2006, June 1). Everand. https://www.everand.com/book/165881699/Man-s-Search-for-Meaning

Marcus Aurelius (Stanford Encyclopedia of Philosophy). (2017, December 22). https://plato.stanford.edu/entries/marcus-aurelius/

Mark, J. J. (2023). Zeno of Citium. World History Encyclopedia. https://www.worldhistory.org/Zeno_of_Citium/

Nair, S. (2023, September 25). Stoic Journaling - How to Apply the Philosophy of Stoicism into Your Journaling Journey Blog. https://blog.journey.cloud/stoic-journaling-how-to-apply-the-philosophy-of-stoicism-into-your-journaling/

Nash, J., Ph.D. (2023, October 13). ACT therapy techniques: 14+ interventions for your sessions. PositivePsychology.com. https://positivepsychology.com/act-techniques/

Olsson, J. (2023, November 22). 10 Immortal quotes about Money by the wealthy stoic Seneca. Medium. https://medium.com/change-becomes-you/10-immortal-quotes-about-money-by-the-wealthy-stoic-seneca-133b9a051f6a

Ontiveros, C. (2023, February 23). The Four Pillars of Stoicism. Stoa Conversations: Stoicism Applied. https://stoameditation.com/blog/the-four-pillars-of-stoicism/

Park, D. (2023, August 19). Reflections on Marcus Aurelius: Discipline, emotion, and growth. Medium. https://medium.com/@pdoeunMind/reflections-on-marcus-aurelius-discipline-emotion-and-growth-a7d9affa51f3

Popova, M. (2018, November 13). Seneca on true and false friendship. The Marginalian. https://www.themarginalian.org/2017/05/19/seneca-friendship/

Reporter, G. S. (2018, October 17). The lost art of concentration: being distracted in a digital world. The Guardian. https://www.theguardian.com/lifeandstyle/2018/oct/14/the-lost-art-of-concentration-being-distracted-in-a-digital-world

Robertson, D. J. (2021a, December 11). Stoic Philosophy as a Cognitive-Behavioral Therapy - Stoicism — Philosophy as a way of life - medium. Medium. https://medium.com/stoicism-philosophy-as-a-way-of-life/stoic-philosophy-as-a-cognitive-behavioral-therapy-597fbeba786a

Robertson, D. J. (2021b, December 27). The Stoicism of George Washington - Stoicism — Philosophy as a way of life - medium. Medium. https://medium.com/stoicism-philosophy-as-a-way-of-life/the-stoicism-of-george-washington-bee78ec0a9e4

Saluja, K. (2023, November 19). The Impact of Perception: Unraveling Epictetus's insight on emotional resilience. Medium. https://medium.-

com/@kulwantsaluja/the-impact-of-perception-unraveling-epictetuss-insight-on-emotional-resilience-1fa3040d28ca

Seneca (Stanford Encyclopedia of Philosophy). (2020, January 15). https://plato.stanford.edu/entries/seneca/

Stoic Ethics | Internet Encyclopedia of Philosophy. (n.d.-a). https://iep.utm.edu/stoiceth/

Stoic Ethics | Internet Encyclopedia of Philosophy. (n.d.-b). https://iep.utm.edu/stoiceth/

Stoicism | Definition, History, & Influence. (2024, January 2). Encyclopedia Britannica. https://www.britannica.com/topic/Stoicism/Stoicism-in-medieval-and-modern-philosophy

Stoicism and its influence on Roman life and thought on JSTOR. (n.d.). www.jstor.org. https://www.jstor.org/stable/3289820

Stoicism (Stanford Encyclopedia of Philosophy). (2023a, January 20). https://plato.stanford.edu/entries/stoicism/

Stoicism (Stanford Encyclopedia of Philosophy). (2023b, January 20). https://plato.stanford.edu/entries/stoicism/

Stoicism, W. I. (2023, April 17). 9 Stoic Journal Prompts — a simple approach to daily journaling. Medium. https://medium.com/stoicism-philosophy-as-a-way-of-life/9-stoic-journal-prompts-a-simple-approach-to-daily-journaling-a0022b1c1bc0

The Stoic Dichotomy of Control in Practice - Psychology Today. (n.d.). https://www.psychologytoday.com/us/blog/365-ways-to-be-more-stoic/202304/the-stoic-dichotomy-of-control-in-practice#:~:text=The%20Stoics%20thought%20that%20there,is%20outside%20our%20direct%20control.

Weaver, T. (2022, August 2). Stoicism and relationships. Orion Philosophy. https://www.orionphilosophy.com/stoic-blog/stoicism-and-relationships

Weaver, T. (2023, November 14). The stoic virtue of justice. Orion Philosophy. https://www.orionphilosophy.com/stoic-blog/the-stoic-virtue-of-justice#:~:text=Justice%20and%20Modern%20Applications,ethical%20action%20and%20social%20reform.

Whitworth, E. (2023, January 3). How to face challenges in life: Stoic advice from Epictetus. Shortform Books. https://www.shortform.com/blog/how-to-face-challenges-in-life/

Wittkowski, P. (2023, November 16). Unlocking Timeless Wisdom: How Marcus Aurelius' meditations can guide the modern aspiring youth. Medium. https://medium.com/@pwittmedia/unlocking-timeless-wisdom-how-marcus-aurelius-meditations-can-guide-the-modern-aspiring-youth-030c08a252a8

Work-focused cognitive behavioral intervention for . . . (n.d.). Ncbi. https://www.ncbi.nlm.nih.gov/pmc/articles/PMC5567478/

Atkins, C. (2017, March 6). No Man is Free Who is Not Master of Himself. Neologikon. Retrieved from https://neologikonblog.wordpress.com/2017/03/06/no-man-is-free-who-is-not-master-of-himyself/

Epictetus Quotes. (n.d.). BrainyQuote.com. Retrieved December 25, 2023, from BrainyQuote.com Web site: https://www.brainyquote.com/quotes/epictetus_149126

Epictetus & Lebell, S. (1995). The Art of Living: The Classical Manual on Virtue, Happiness, and Effectiveness [PDF]. HarperOne.

Haakonssen, K. (Ed.). (2008). The meditations of the Emperor Marcus Aurelius Antoninus (J. Moore & M. Silverthorne, Eds.). Liberty Fund.

Popova, M. (2014). The Shortness of Life: Seneca on Busyness and the Art of Living Wide Rather Than Living Long. Retrieved from https://www.themarginalian.org/2014/09/01/seneca-on-the-shortness-of-life/

Sellars, J. (2019, November 26). Lessons from Seneca. Who was Lucius Annaeus Seneca? On one... Stoicism — Philosophy as a Way of Life. Medium. Retrieved from https://medium.com/stoicism-philosophy-as-a-way-of-life/lessons-from-seneca-d9e2bb02fdb4

Seneca & Campbell, R. A. (1969). Letters from a Stoic: Epistulae Morales ad Lucilium [PDF]. Penguin Books.

Wilson, E. (2015). Seneca, the fat-cat philosopher. The Guardian. Retrieved from https://www.theguardian.com/books/2015/mar/27/seneca-fat-cat-philosopher-emily-wilson-a-life.

www.ingramcontent.com/pod-product-compliance
Lightning Source LLC
Chambersburg PA
CBHW030439010526
44118CB00011B/707